Catholic Study Guides for Mary Fabyan Windeatt's

Saint Rose,
First Canonized Saint of the Americas

Saint Martin de Porres,
The Story of the Little Doctor of Lima, Peru

King David and His Songs,
A Story of the Psalms

Blessed Marie of New France,
The Story of the First Missionary Sisters in Canada

RACE for Heaven's Grade 5 Study Guides

Janet P. McKenzie

Biblio Resource Publications, Inc.
Bessemer, Michigan

Saint Rose of Lima Study Guide © 2001 by Janet P. McKenzie
Saint Martin de Porres Study Guide © 2001 by Janet P. McKenzie
King David and His Songs Study Guide © 2004 by Janet P. McKenzie
Blessed Marie of New France Study Guide © 2004 by Janet P. McKenzie

Catholic Study Guides for Mary Fabyan Windeatt's Saints Grade 5 © 2007 by Janet P. McKenzie

ISBN 978-1-934185-07-0
Second printing 2015

Published by Biblio Resource Publications, Inc.
108 ½ South Moore Street
Bessemer, MI 49911
info@BiblioResource.com
www.BiblioResource.com

A **R**ead **A**loud **C**urriculum **E**nrichment Product
www.RACEforHeaven.com

All right reserved. With the exception of short excerpts for critical reviews, no part of this work may be reproduced or transmitted in any form or by any means whatsoever without the written permission of the publisher.

Cover photo of Obelisk and Basilica in St. Peters Square, Rome © iofoto - Fotolia.com

Special thanks to Julia Fogassy from Our Father's House for her editorial assistance

Scripture texts in this work are taken from the New American Bible, revised edition © 2010, 1991, 1986, 1970 Confraternity of Christian Doctrine, Washington, D.C. and are used by permission of the copyright owner. All Rights Reserved. No part of the New American Bible may be reproduced in any form without permission in writing from the copyright owner.

All quotations from the Windeatt biographies are excerpted from the edition published by Tan Books and Publisher, Inc. If using the original hardback version of these books, note that the text will be the same but the page numbers will vary from the Tan edition.

Printed in the United States of America

Table of Contents

Spiritual Read Aloud .... i-iv
How to Use These Study Guides .... v-vii

Saint Rose of Lima 1-16
    Poetic Summary of the Life of St. Rose of Lima   1
    Timeline of Events Surrounding the Life of St. Rose of Lima   2
    Map of the World of St. Rose of Lima   3
    Saints of the Americas   4
    Catholic Enrichment Activities for Chapters 1 through 13   5-12
    Book Summary Test for *Saint Rose of Lima*   13-14
    Answer Key for Comprehension Questions and Book Summary Test   15-16

Saint Martin de Porres 17-40
    Poetic Summary of the Life of St. Martin de Porres   17
    Timeline of Events Surrounding the Life of St. Martin de Porres   18
    Map of the World of St. Martin de Porres   19
    Catholic Enrichment Activities for Chapters 1 through 13   21-33
    Martin's Works of Mercy   34
    Book Summary Test for *Saint Martin de Porres*   35-36
    Answer Key for Comprehension Questions and Book Summary Test 37-39

King David and His Songs 41-60
    Poetic Summary of the Life of King David   41
    Timeline of Events Surrounding the Life of King David   42
    The Kingdom of King David   43
    Catholic Enrichment Activities for Chapters 1—20   45-53
    Kings and Prophets of the United and Divided Kingdoms   54
    Book Summary Test for *King David and His Songs*   55-56
    Answer Key for Comprehension Questions and Book Summary Test   57-59
    Note on Personal and Geographical Names in the Bible   60

Blessed Marie of New France 61-82
    Poetic Summary of the Life of Blessed Marie of New France   61
    Timeline of Events Surrounding the Life of Blessed Marie of New France   62
    Map of Blessed Marie's France   63
    Catholic Enrichment Activities for Chapters 1 through 11   65-75
    A Pilgrim's Prayer (Shrine of Saint Anne in Beaupré)   76
    Book Summary Test for *Blessed Marie of New France*   77-78
    Answer Key for Comprehension Questions and Book Summary Test   79-81

Other RACE for Heaven Products 83-88

Spiritual Read Aloud

Spiritual Reading

In *My Daily Bread, A Summary of the Spiritual Life* by Father Anthony Paone, S.J., Christ tells us,

> My Child, reading and reflecting are a great help to your spiritual life. My doctrine is explained in many books. . . . Some of these books are written simply, and some are very profound and learned. Choose those which will help you most toward a greater understanding and appreciation of My Truth. Do not read to impress others but rather to be impressed yourself. Read so that you may learn My way of thinking and of doing things.

In her book, *Saint Dominic, Preacher of the Rosary and Founder of the Dominican Order*, Mary Fabyan Windeatt quotes St. Dominic as saying, "A little good reading, much prayer and meditation . . . and God will do the rest." Father Peter-Thomas Rohrbach, O.C.D., states that spiritual reading is the "third essential asset for mediation" (after detachment and recollection). The great value he places on the habit of spiritual reading is expressed in his book *Conversation with Christ, An Introduction to Mental Prayer*:

> We live in a world devoid, in great part, of a Christian spirit, in an atmosphere and culture estranged from God. Living in such a non-theological environment makes it difficult for us to remain in contact with the person of Christ and the true purpose of life itself. We must, if we are to remain realistically attached to Christ, combat this atmosphere and surround ourselves with a new one. Constant spiritual reading fills our minds with Christ and His doctrine—it creates this new climate for us.
>
> In former ages, spiritual reading was not as essential for one's prayer life. People lived in a Christian world and culture which was reflected in their laws, customs, amusements, and their very outlook on life. This situation has radically altered in the last two hundred years, and men must now compensate for this deficit through other media, principally reading. And as the de-Christianization of our world continues, the necessity for spiritual reading simultaneously increases. We stand in need of something to bridge the gap between our pagan surroundings and our conversation with Christ—spiritual reading fills this need.
>
> There is today in our country an alarming decline in general reading of all types. It has been estimated that in 1955 an astonishing forty-eight percent of the American adult population reads *no books at all*, and only eighteen percent read from one to four books. The decline in reading is naturally reflected in religious reading as well. And, while the lack of secular reading will occasion a decrease in culture life, the decline in religious reading

will have repercussions of a more serious nature—severe detriment to one's spiritual life. Any serious attempt to better one's life spiritually should, therefore, include the resolution to engage in more spiritual reading.

If we confine our reading to non-Catholic books, magazines and newspapers, we almost automatically exclude ourselves from full development in our prayer life. The maxims and philosophy of life expressed in these avenues of communication slowly begin to seep into our lives until eventually they occupy a ruling position. We will not have surrounded ourselves with a new climate; rather, the non-Catholic climate will have engulfed us.

As this decry of the "de-Christianization of our world" was written in 1956, one can safely surmise that the necessity of cultivating the habit of spiritual reading can only have grown in the past several decades.

Spiritual Read Aloud

As supported above, spiritual reading is an essential element of every Christian's life. However, as demonstrated by the ancient practice within monasteries of spiritual read-aloud, this habit is a powerful tool for shared community growth in the spiritual life. For Catholic families, the practice of reading spiritual books aloud produces four desirable effects:

I. It reinforces the habit of spiritual reading for each member of the family and allows each member to practice this habit regardless of age.

II. It reinforces the habit of spiritual conversation if the reading results in even a general discussion of the values and virtues being portrayed in the story.

III. It strengthens the family as the domestic Church where members exist to learn and live the Faith together for the support and enrichment of all family members.

IV. It allows the discussion and demonstration of the practical application of the Faith for all age levels.

The Habit of Spiritual Reading

As outlined above, establishing the habit of daily spiritual reading is essential to our spiritual growth. Through read-aloud, children can be taught at an early age that daily spiritual reading is a fun, rewarding exercise. Do make this time together pleasant by allowing the children to do crafts, draw, play quietly with puzzles, toys, etc. As long as their attention is not divided and they can participate in a discussion of the reading afterwards, allow quiet activity. One cannot expect children to sit piously with hands clasped prayerfully throughout the read-aloud session! As the children get older, encourage them to read other spiritual books, including the Bible, during a quiet time of their own. Model this habit by allowing them to observe your habit of daily spiritual reading as well. Although the family read-aloud sessions may be as long as thirty minutes, private spiritual reading times may be considerably shorter depending on the habits and temperament of each child.

The Habit of Spiritual Conversation

This habit, for many families, may begin with spiritual read-aloud. When each member of the family participates in a spiritual discussion of a religious book, the practice of discussing matters of faith and Christ-like living begins to form. If the formation of holy habits and imitation of the saints is the goal, these discussions will become commonplace in the home as each member checks the others on their actions and words. As family members become more comfortable and open about spiritual matters, this practice will soon spread into other areas of their lives. Spiritual discussions with friends and other relatives will become more natural and in fact become important topics to be discussed. Sharing one's own spirituality and encouraging others to become more open about matters of faith will then become an integral pattern of living.

Strengthening the Domestic Church

As we read more about the saints and their lives and begin to share our faith more openly with others, we realize the importance of holy companionship—living with others who share our faith ideas and supporting each other in our attempts to become more like Christ. Families begin to grow together in their knowledge of the Catholic faith and become more willing to support each other throughout the ups and downs of community living. We begin to "bear one another's burdens with peace and harmony and unselfishness." Just as Christ has His Church to help bring salvation to all, we—as family members—have each other to provide mutual support and encouragement in our efforts to enter the narrow gate. Within our families, we can create the Catholic culture that is missing from our world's culture.

The Practical Application of the Faith for All Age Levels

When lives of the saints are read aloud in the family setting, all aged children can participate in a discussion of the imitation of the saint's virtues and holy habits. Each member can help others understand how to apply the lessons the saints teach us on a practical level. All family members can help choose a particular habit or virtue upon which to focus. A reward system can be established for virtuous behavior. A family "plan of attack" on non-virtuous habits and attitudes can be developed, implemented, checked, and revised. All members can be encouraged and taught to imitate Christ by the imitation of His saints.

Summary

Regular family read-loud sessions that center around the lives of the saints will benefit the family with an increased interest in reading—especially saintly literature, a growth in vocabulary, and an improved sense of family unity. Additionally, family members will be encouraged to develop the habit of spiritual reading on their own, will become more comfortable and experienced with spiritual conversation, and be able to apply the Truths of the Catholic faith, on a practical level, to all aspects of their lives—no matter what their age. The customs, habits, and attitudes of the family will more and more reflect those of the Catholic culture. Perseverance in this simple daily ritual will help to "bridge the gap between our pagan surroundings and our conversation with Christ."

When Mother Reads Aloud

When Mother reads aloud the past
Seems real as every day;
I hear the tramp of armies vast,
I see the spears and lances cast,
I join the thrilling fray;
Brave knights and ladies fair and proud
I meet when Mother reads aloud.

When Mother reads aloud, far lands
Seem very near and true;
I cross the desert's gleaming sands,
Or hunt the jungle's prowling bands,
Or sail the ocean blue;
Far heights, whose peaks the cold mists
   shroud,
I scale, when Mother reads aloud.

When Mother reads aloud I long
For noble deeds to do—
To help the right, redress the wrong,
It seems so easy to be strong, so simple
   to be true,
O, thick and fast the visions crowd
When Mother reads aloud.
–*Anonymous*

The Reading Mother

I had a mother who read to me
Sagas of pirates who scoured the sea,
Cutlasses clenched in their yellow teeth,
"Blackbirds" stowed in the hold beneath.

I had a mother who read me plays
Of ancient and gallant and golden days
Stories of Marmion and Ivanhoe,
Which every boy has a right to know.

I had a mother who read me tales
Of Gelert, the hound of the hills of
   Wales,
True to his trust till his tragic death,
Faithfulness blest with his final breath.

I had a mother who read me things
That wholesome life to the boy-heart
   brings—
Stories that stir with an upward touch,
O, that each mother of boys were such.

You may have tangible wealth untold,
Caskets of jewels and coffers of gold.
Richer than I you can never be—
I had a mother who read to me.
–*Strickland Gullilan*

How to Use These Study Guides

⭐REVIEW⭐ Vocabulary

Vocabulary words are listed at the beginning of each lesson. Words on the left are secular words and are given within the sentence structure. Allow students to guess the meaning of the italicized word before looking it up. This helps them to surmise the meaning from context, a skill that enhances reading comprehension and strengthens vocabulary. Vocabulary words listed in the right-hand column are Catholic vocabulary words. Help students identify any suffixes, prefixes or root words that might give clues to the word's meaning. To help with definitions and proper usage, use a dictionary. For Catholic vocabulary words, use a Catholic encyclopedia, dictionary, or catechism.

??? Comprehension Questions/Narration Prompts

These questions are appropriate for all age levels. They can be used several ways, depending on a student's ability. For students with difficulty in reading comprehension, read and briefly discuss these questions before reading the chapter. Discuss, too, the sub-title provided under each chapter heading in the study guide. The student will then know what content to watch for within the reading. If read afterward, the questions become a *test of,* rather than an *aid to,* comprehension. For students with adequate comprehension skills, use the questions for oral review after the reading to insure that important content has been absorbed.

Use these questions too as prompts for narration, which is simply the oral retelling of the story in the student's own words. It is a helpful tool to determine the level of each student's comprehension. All ages may benefit from the practice of narration. If done within a mixed age group, begin with the youngest students and have the older students add details to the already-related story.

Answers to comprehension questions are provided in the answer key.

Forming Opinions/Drawing Conclusions

More than relating events, these questions require the student to develop an opinion, or to uncover or discover material not expressly stated in the text. They are designed to develop thinking skills and do not usually require the use of any outside resources. Use this section with children grades five and up as the basis for discussion or as a writing assignment.

For Further Study

Appropriate for upper elementary through high school grades, this section requires the use of additional reference materials. These activities invite students to look more deeply at the historical events and people that shaped the times of each character. Topics in this section may be used for honing research skills, or for oral presentations and/or written reports.

Growing in Holiness

These activities are different from the others in that they do not involve discussion or study as much as personal action and interior reflection. They can perhaps be considered "conversion activities" or "life lessons." By applying the spiritual lessons of the story to everyday life, the student is encouraged to develop habits in imitation of the saints—which is an imitation of Christ Himself. Remember to reinforce these activities with the student and to comment when they are observed in action.

 Geography

The map provided with this study guide serves to orient the students with respect to space—*where* the action of the story is taking place—as well as to acquaint them with common geographical landmarks. Permission is hereby granted to photocopy maps for family or classroom use.

 Timeline Work

The creation of a timeline allows students to place the story's events within a wider historical framework. Simple directions for making a timeline are included in the study guide. Students will need plain paper, colored markers, and a ruler.

✓ **Checking the Catechism**

For older students, these activities require a copy of the *Catechism of the Catholic Church* (*CCC*) or its *Compendium*. The references for the more concise *Compendium* appear in parentheses after the *CCC* citations. Older students can read aloud—and then discuss—the stated text paragraphs with an adult.

For younger students, use any grade-appropriate catechism to review the doctrines and terms as specified. An excellent activity book for multi-grades is Ignatius Press' *100 Activities Based on the Catechism of the Catholic Church* by Ellen Rossini. Discuss together how the specific topics from the catechism are illustrated in the thoughts and actions of the characters in the book.

 Searching Scripture

Familiarize the student with the inspired Word of God by studying the biblical passages provided. Strengthen these exercises by occasionally requiring memorization of the verse(s). Stress that knowledge of Scripture is an important part of our faith education.

Note that Ms. Windeatt used the Douay-Rheims translation of the Bible, which was the translation in use in the United States until 1970 when it was replaced by the New American Bible in the *Lectionary of Mass*. The Douay-Rheims translation is taken from the Latin Vulgate, whereas the New American translation comes from the original languages of Hebrew, Aramaic or Greek (as the case may be for each specific book). For this reason, some of the books' names (as well as some of the Psalms' numbers) differ between these two translations. When these differences occur in the biblical citiations within this study guide, the New American references are given first with the Douay-Rheims references following in parentheses. All biblical references used in this study guide are from the New American translation.

 **Test**

The purpose of the test is to ensure that the student has comprehended the important events in each saint's life as well as the lessons the story intends to impart. An answer key is provided for these questions.

In addition to the test, many students will benefit from the completion of a book report. See RACE for Heaven's *Alternative Book Reports for Catholic Students* for additional information on book reports specifically geared toward saint biographies. Consider requiring each student to choose one of these reports or activities upon completion of the Windeatt biography.

Warning

These study guides are comprehensive. They contain activities for a variety of age levels and areas of study. Do **not** attempt to complete every activity for every lesson. Do only those exercises that are suitable for the needs of your current situation. Resist the impulse to be so thorough that the story line of the book is lost, and the read-aloud sessions become dreaded rather than anticipated. The activities are designed to enhance your reading—not to become the dictating tyrant of your read-aloud time together. If you are using these guides for young audiences, consider just using the comprehension and opinion questions as well as the "Growing in Holiness" section; use the maps as a geographical visual aid. Re-read the books to complete the more advanced activities in later years.

Another suggestion is to use the activities designed for older students in coordination with their history, geography, writing and/or religious curriculum. Each study guide could also be used as a complete unit study for hectic times when regular school may not be in session such as Advent, times of family stress (the birth of a new sibling, for example) or over the summer months. In reading the book and completing the activities, subjects such as religion, reading, writing, geography, and history can all be easily covered.

The most important rules to the successful use of these enrichment activities are
1. Be creative rather than obsessive.
2. Be flexible rather than overly structured.
3. Enjoy

Study Guide for

Saint Rose of Lima, The Story of the First Canonized Saint of the Americas

St. Rose of Lima

First saint of America—St. Rose was her name.
Though Isabel at birth, Rose was her nickname.
She learned how to pray.
God showed her His way—
Taught her music and reading—writing just came.

Turribius confirmed Rose at eleven.
The Gifts of the Spirit, she got all seven.
She worked and she played—
Sacrifices were made;
She wanted to pray, suffer, save souls for heaven.

Father Francis Solonus preached a great speech,
He talked about pride—simple love he did teach.
Her mother and Rose
Their doors did not close
But opened them up, to others did reach.

Augustinian, Dominican, Poor Clare—
Which one? Everyone had a thought to declare.
But no nun for her,
And none could deter,
Her life as a hermit, the poor in her care.

She helped where she could. Flowers were her thing.
As a special sign, God gave her a ring.
In the world still,
God's will to fulfill.
To the life of a hermit she continued to cling.

Wonders performed, the enemy withdrew.
She moved in with friends, her poor health to renew.
Her own death predicts,
The very day picks
The feast of Bartholomew in Lima, Peru.

Think what you can learn from this saint and her tale.
How you can apply it to help you prevail.
Then mold what you do
And boldly pursue
Her pattern of holiness. Follow her trail.

Timeline of Events

Year	Event
1517	Protestant Reformation begins in Europe with Martin Luther
1521	Herman Cortez conquers Aztec empire
1526	Founding of the Mogul Muslim Empire, Kabul (now Afghanistan)
1533	Francisco Pizarro captures the Inca capital, Cuzco and conquers Peru
1534	St. Ignatius of Loyola founds the Society of Jesus
1535	Large silver mines discovered in Peru and Mexico
1543	Copernicus publishes his theory that the earth revolves around the sun
1545-63	First Council of Trent held as called by Pope Paul III
1549	St. Francis Xavier arrives in Japan as a missionary
1551	Founding of the first university in the New World at Lima, Peru
1562	French Wars of Religion begin
1564	Birth of William Shakespeare; death of John Calvin
1567	City of Rio de Janeiro, Argentina, founded
1571	Mediterranean Sea Battle of Lepanto fought; sugar plantations set up in Brazil
1573	Birth of Michelangelo Caravaggio
1575	Plague sweeps through Italy and Sicily
1577	Sir Francis Drake sets out to sail around the world
1579	Birth of St. Martin de Porres
1582	Introduction of the Gregorian Calendar, named for Pope Gregory XIII
1586	Birth of St. Rose Flores in Lima, Peru; Jesuits found missions in Paraguay
1587	Death of Mary, Queen of Scots
1588	Defeat of the Spanish Armada
1590	First microscope made by Hans and Zacharias Janssen
1597	Sacrament of Confirmation given to Rose
1604	Father Francis Solano preaches famous sermon causing thousands to confess
1605	Publication of *Don Quixote* by Miguel de Cervantes
1606	Archbishop Turribius dies; Rose joins the Dominican Order as a tertiary; Australia discovered by the Dutch
1610	Rose receives her golden ring and builds her hermitage; first telescope observations made by Galileo
1611	Publication of the King James Bible
1615	Rose leaves home to live with Don and Dona Maria Gonzalo
1617	Death of St. Rose of Lima who was canonized in 1671; Sir Walter Raleigh leads expedition to South American to find El Dorado
1618	Beginning of the Thirty Years' War in Europe
1620	Pilgrims land near Cape Cod
1633	Death of Sister Maria of Saint Mary, St. Rose's mother
1639	Death of St. Martin de Porres
1642	Birth of Isaac Newton
1650	Completion of the *Taj Mahal* in Arga, India
1654	Portuguese drive Dutch from Brazil
1678	John Bunyan publishes *Pilgrim's Progress*

Saints of the Americas (List current as of January 2015)

1. St. Rose of Lima (1671, Peru)
2. St. Francis Solano (1726, Peru)
3. St. Turibuis de Mogrovejo (1726, Peru)
4. St. Francis Blanco, companion to Paul Miki (1862, Mexico)
5. St. Francis de San Miguel, companion to Paul Miki (1862, Mexico)
6. St. Martin de Aguirre, companion to Paul Miki (1862, Mexico)
7. St. Peter Baptist Blasquez, companion to Paul Miki (1862, Mexico)
8. St. Philip of Jesus de las Casas, companion to Paul Miki (1862, Mexico)
9. St. Peter Claver (1888, Columbia)
10. Eight North American martyrs—Isaac Jogues and René Goupil, died in the United States; John de Lalande, John de Brébeuf, Anthony Daniel, Gabriel Lalemant, Charles Garnier, and Noel Chabanel, died in Canada (1930)
11. St. Frances Xavier Cabrini (1946, United States)
12. St. Anthony Mary Claret (1950, Cuba)
13. St. Mariana of Jesus Paredes y Flores, or "The Lily of Quirto" (1950, Ecuador)
14. St. Martin de Porres (1962, Peru)
15. St. Elizabeth Ann Seton (1975, United States)
16. St. John Masias (1975, Peru)
17. St. John Neumann (1977, United States)
18. St. Marguerite Bourgeoys (1982, Canada)
19. St. Miguel Febres Cordero (1984, Ecuador)
20. St. Alphonse Rodriguez (1988, Paraguay)
21. St. John de Castillo (1988, Paraguay)
22. St. Roque (Roch) Gonzalez (1988, Paraguay)
23. St. Rose Philippine Duchesne (1988, United States)
24. St. Marie Marguerite D'Youville (1990, Canada)
25. St. Ezequiel Moreño y Diaz (1992, Dominican Republic)
26. St. Teresa Fernandez Solar, or Teresa of the Andes (1993, Chili)
27. 25 martyrs including twenty-one priests and three laymen (2000, Mexico)
28. St. José María de Yermo y Parres (2000, Mexico)
29. St. Katharine Drexel (2000, United States)
30. St. María de Jesus Sacramentado (2000, Mexico)
31. St. Juan Diego (2002, Mexico)
32. St. Paolina (Pauline) of the Heart of Jesus in Agony (2002, Brazil)
33. St. Pedro de San José Betancur (2002, Guatemala)
34. St. Alberto Hurtado Cruchaga (2005, Chili)
35. St. Theodore Guerin (2006, United States)
36. St. Rafael Guizar Valencia (2006, Mexico)
37. St. Antonio Galvao (2007, Brazil)
38. St. Maria Bernard (Verena) Bütler (2008, Ecuador and Columbia)
39. St. Narcisa de Jesús Martillo Morán (2008, Ecuador)
40. St. Kateri Tekakwitha (2012, United States and Canada)
41. St. Maria Guadalupe García Zavala (2013, Mexico)
42. St. Laura di Santa Caterina da Siena Montoya y Upegui (2013, Columbia)
43. St. María Guadalupe "Lupita" García Zavala (2013, Mexico)
44. St. José de Anchieta y Díaz de Clavijo (2014, Brazil)
45. St. Marie of the Incarnation (2014, Canada)
46. St. Francis-Xavier de Montmorency-Laval (2014, Canada)

Chapters 1 and 2—In Which Rose Is Born, Named, Learns to Read, and Receives the Sacrament of Confirmation

 Vocabulary

the little silky *vicunas*
alpacas with their shaggy brown coats
catechism
Chrism

 Comprehension Questions/Narration Prompts
1. What is the ongoing argument between Rose's mother and grandmother?
2. On whose feast day was Rose born?
3. Why does the Flores family move to Quivi?
4. At what age does Rose receive the Sacrament of Confirmation and from whom?

 For Further Study
The statue of the Christ Child, with a robe of its own, is mentioned several times. Research the history of the Infant of Prague, a traditional Spanish devotion, as well as the chaplet and novena prayer associated with this statue.

 Growing in Holiness
Rose's mother tells Rose that there is only one thing that is really important: knowing what is good and doing it (page 5). Examine each action today to insure that it is good and that, in fact, you are doing only those things that are good.

 Geography
Using the map found on page 3 of this study guide, trace the outline of the map as well as the boundary lines of the countries. Label and color the seas, as well as the Amazon River, blue. Using the inset map, note the continent's world position. (The remainder of the map will be completed in Chapters 7 and 8.)

✓ **Checking the Catechism**
Older students may read about the Christian name in the *Catechism of the Catholic Church* (*CCC*) in text paragraphs 2156-59 and 2165 (264). Review the summary of Baptism in text paragraphs 1275-1284. Younger students may review Baptism in their own catechisms. If desired, complete Activity #11 and/or Activity #87 in *100 Activities Based on the Catechism of the Catholic Church* (*100 Activities*).

 Searching Scripture
"He (God) would listen to her, as He had done about the reading and writing, just because she was so weak and helpless" (page 11). Read the following list of Bible passages dealing with spiritual childhood: Psalm 116 (114):6, Psalm 119 (118):130, Wisdom 6:7, Isaiah (Isaias) 66: 12-13, Matthew 18:1-5, and Mark 10:14-15.

Chapters 3 and 4—In Which Rose Prays and Suffers to Save Souls, and Confides in Doctor John and Dona Maria

 Vocabulary

were gathering *menacingly*
Wretched *pagans*

mitre (or *miter*)
blessing

 Comprehension Questions/Narration Prompts
1. What was "the secret" of Chapter 3?
2. Who does Doctor John tell Rose of—someone about her age who lives in Lima and who is also very interested in saving souls?
3. Why does Rose not enjoy entertaining many of her mother's guests?

 Forming Opinions/Drawing Conclusions
Rose states, "No one could pray too much" (page 31). Make a list of some holy habits that you could acquire that might make someone be concerned that you pray too much.

 For Further Study
Several other members of the Dominican order who later were canonized as saints of the Church lived in Lima at the same time as Rose. Research the lives of Martin de Porres, Turribius Alphonsius de Mogrovejo, and John Masias, as well as the Franciscan friar Francis Solano—all contemporaries of Rose.

 Growing in Holiness
Rose "could think of no material way to help the thousands of wretched Indians and Negroes. She could only continue to offer small sacrifices to God the Father, uniting them to the sufferings of Christ on earth and asking that He bless the natives in their poverty and ignorance" (page 25). Adopt a group of people—such as those afflicted with an addiction, the unborn, or those who suffer the effects of war. Make sacrifices each day and recite special prayers for this group. Use a set of beads to keep track of these sacrifices, as did St. Therese, the Little Flower.

✓ **Checking the Catechism**
Rose expresses her excitement that she can now "grow up with the help of four wonderful Sacraments" (page 19). Review the seven sacraments. Make sure these can be listed from memory. Older students may read the following text paragraphs from the *CCC*: 1210-13, 1285, 1322-23, 1420-22, 1499, 1533-36, and 1601-02 (224-232, 248-250, 354, 357).

Chapters 5 and 6—In Which Rose Visits the Monasteries of Lima, and Francis Solano Comes to Preach

 Vocabulary

thick *adobe* wall *Tertiary*
It's a *pioneer* venture *hermitage*

 Comprehension Questions/Narration Prompts
1. Why does Rose wish she were a boy?
2. What stories do Rose and Dona Maria share on the way to the monastery?
3. What is the message of Francis Solano's sermon that causes Rose's mother to welcome the injured Indian woman into her home?

 Forming Opinions/Drawing Conclusions
Expand on Dona Maria's comment, "It takes a very special grace to become a saint while you go on living in the world" (page 38).

 Growing in Holiness
"I promised Our Lord that I would always love Him more than anyone or anything" (page 40). We are commanded by the first commandment to love and serve God above all things. Do a mental inventory to see if there are any things, people, or habits in your life that put God in second place. Should you find any that seem more important than God, decide what you can do to correct your priorities.

 Timeline Work
Taping sheets of plain paper end-to-end, make a timeline representing the years from 1517 through 1678. Let three inches equal 25 years. Mark on your timeline the dates and events from 1517 through 1582, using information from page 2 of this study guide.

✓ **Checking the Catechism**
St. Rose of Lima is quoted twice in the *CCC*. The first is a reference to her sentiment on the Cross, and the second refers to our need to serve. Read these quotations in text paragraphs 618 and 2449.

📖 **Searching Scripture**
Read Hebrews 12:1-13 on remaining firm in our faith and showing a willingness to suffer as Christ did.

Chapters 7 and 8—In Which Don Gonzalo Resolves to Help Rose Become a Poor Clare Nun, and Rose is Unable to Leave Santo Domingo to Join the Augustinian Convent

★REVIEW★ Vocabulary
ragged *urchins*
supply his daughter with a *dowry*
Poor Clares
Vespers

??? Comprehension Questions/Narration Prompts
1. Who is "The Little Doctor"?
2. What signs does Martin de Porres state as possible evidence that the saintly bishop Turribius had gone straight to heaven upon his death?
3. Why did Rose hesitate to join any of the five convents in the city of Lima?
4. Why was Rose unable to leave the Dominican church to go to the Augustinian convent?

 Forming Opinions/Drawing Conclusions

Put yourself in Rose's place. Imagine the pressure from her parents (especially her mother), Don Gonzalo, and Dona Maria to marry or to join a convent. What might you have done under similar circumstances?

 Growing in Holiness

Don Gonzalo "suffered a distraction" at Mass (page 62). Concentrate on being more attentive at Mass so as not to "suffer a distraction" yourself. Remember what each Mass commemorates and the significance of the Sacrifice.

 Geography

Complete the map started in Chapters 1 and 2 by marking the names of the countries and cities; label the cities red and the countries in green. On the map provided, seas are in italics, cities are indicated with a star, and countries are in bold capitals. Add too the Equator and the Andes Mountains. If you are already familiar with the South American countries, try to label them on your own.

 Timeline Work

Add the dates and events from 1586 through 1606 to your timeline.

 Searching Scripture

Rose felt that to care for the sick "was to love Our Lord" (page 55). Find at least four Scripture passages that show Jesus caring for the sick.

Saint Rose of Lima 9

Chapter 9—In Which Rose Becomes a Spouse of Christ

 Vocabulary

who didst *vouchsafe*
sprinkle thee with *hyssop*

cloister
Repository

 Comprehension Questions/Narration Prompts
1. What name did Rose take when she became a Dominican tertiary?
2. Where did Rose find relief for her lonely heart?
3. Why did Rose want a ring? What was to be the inscription on this ring?

 Forming Opinions/Drawing Conclusions
"We can only be satisfied with the greatest good of all—God Himself" (page 80). In his *Confessions*, Saint Augustine states, "Our heart is restless until it rests in You." What can we learn from these two companion thoughts? What changes in your life does this knowledge prompt?

 For Further Study
Re-read the discussion on servants between Rose and her mother on page 79. Jesus said that He did not come to be served but to serve others—Matthew 20:28. Research other Biblical passages that deal with service. Pope St. Gregory called himself "the servant of the servants of God." Write an essay on our need to be servants and to be of service to others.

 Growing in Holiness
Don Gonzalo states, "She is to be a model for all who must reach perfection without the help of the cloister" (page 77). With Rose's life as your model, consider what you can do to imitate her holiness. What habits of hers do you wish to imitate?

✓ **Checking the Catechism**
1. Rose's mother, Maria de Oliva, had planned for Rose to receive the Sacrament of Matrimony (marriage). Older students should read text paragraphs 1655-66 (337-350) in the *CCC*, while younger students review this sacrament in their own catechisms. If desired, complete Activity #91 in *100 Activities*
2. The use of both holy water and blessed palms are mentioned in this chapter. In the *CCC*, read text paragraphs 1667-76 (351-353) on sacramentals, or review sacramentals in your own catechism.

 Searching Scripture
Read in Matthew 21:1-11 of Jesus' entry into Jerusalem on Palm Sunday.

Chapter 10—In Which Rose Builds a Hermitage

 Vocabulary

adobe hermitage
prayer and *petition*

friar
Sanctifying Grace

 Comprehension Questions/Narration Prompts
1. When Rose's mother does not understand her, what does Rose do?
2. What habits of Rose lead others to compare her to St. Catherine of Siena?
3. How does Rose spend her evenings in her hermitage?

 Forming Opinions/Drawing Conclusions
In your own words, explain Rose's description of what sanctifying grace can do in a co-operating soul (page 95). What can you add to her description?

 For Further Study
Study other canonized saints from North and South America—Peru has a total of seven and the United States has nine, excluding the eight North American martyrs. Use the information from "Saints of the Americas" on page 4 of this study guide. Research one of these saints and present your research in a short report or oral presentation.

 Growing in Holiness
With your parent's permission, partition off a portion of your bedroom measuring four feet by five feet. Rose's hermitage was also only six feet high and had one small window. Imagine living in this space permanently as your only living quarters. (Rose's hermitage was out of doors with only a small opening for a doorway.) Remember too that Rose spent each evening in her hermitage praying into the night. Imitate this holy habit for at least one evening. You may use your Bible and other holy books during this meditation time.

✓ **Checking the Catechism**
Rose recalls the night in Lima when there were not enough priests to hear the confessions of all who wished to receive this sacrament (page 87). Older students may read text paragraphs 1422-24, 1430-42, and 1485-98 (295-311) in the *CCC* while younger students review Confession in their catechisms. If desired, complete Activity #61 in *100 Activities*. When is the last time you received this sacrament?

📖 **Searching Scripture**
Rose's mother accuses Rose of turning into a prophet. Read some of the stories of the prophets from the Old Testament. The prophetic books of the Bible start with Isaiah (Isaias) and continue to the end of the Old Testament.

Chapter 11—In Which Rose Moves into the Home of Don Gonzalo and then to Her Heavenly Home

Vocabulary
Couriers kept arriving
there was this *calamity*

Calvinists
Society of Jesus

Comprehension Questions/Narration Prompts
1. Why did Rose wish to be a missionary?
2. Describe some of the activities of Rose in her new home.
3. On what date did Rose of Lima die?

Forming Opinions/Drawing Conclusions
1. Expand on Rose's idea that God gives each of us a kind of martyrdom—one without swords, bullets, or fire (page 105).
2. "Rose had been in love with humility too long" (page 106). What does this mean?

For Further Study
Dona Maria speaks of the Catholic persecution by the Calvinists. Research Calvinism and John Calvin (1509-1564).

Growing in Holiness
"With her rosary in her hand, she would give her life in defense of the Blessed Sacrament" (page 103). Would you? To strengthen your will, begin a practice of reciting short prayers and ejaculations throughout the day (each hour) in imitation of Rose. Some indulgenced ejaculations follow:

My Lord and my God
My God and my all
Holy Mary, pray for us.
Hail, O Cross, our only hope

Jesus, Mary, Joseph
O Lord, increase our faith.
O God, have mercy on me, a sinner.
May the Holy Trinity be blessed.

Sweet Heart of Mary, be my salvation.
Teach me to do your will, because you are my God.
Christ conquers! Christ reigns! Christ commands!
Merciful Lord Jesus, grant them eternal rest.
May the Most Blessed Sacrament be praised and adored forever.
Jesus, meek and humble of heart, make my heart like your Heart.

Searching Scripture
One of Rose's favorite prayers for sinners was from Psalm 70 (69). Read this chapter from the book of Psalms.

Chapters 12 and 13—In Which Peru Pays Its Respects to Rose, and We Learn of Life in Santa Catalina

 Vocabulary

soldiers of the *Viceroy*   *sanctuary*
during the *siesta*   *Pall*

 Comprehension Questions/Narration Prompts
1. List the seven miracles mentioned in these two chapters.
2. Where did Rose wish to be buried? Why was she buried in secret?
3. Why did the convent of Santa Catalina flourish?

 Forming Opinions/Drawing Conclusions
What do you think Rose and her mother might have discussed upon their meeting in heaven after Sister Maria died?

 For Further Study
Research the *Salve Regina* (Hail, Holy Queen). Read on page 137 of Ms. Windeatt's biography, *Saint Hyacinth of Poland, The Story of the Apostle of the North*, how the custom of singing this prayer at the bedside of a dying Dominican began. Find which words of this prayer are commonly attributed to St. Bernard.

 Growing in Holiness
Ask St. Rose to help you in your prayer life. Ask too that she may assist you to live a life of penance, to be willing to make small sacrifices for the salvation of souls, and to obtain a holy zeal for souls. You may wish to compose a short formal prayer to St. Rose for this purpose.

 Timeline Work
Add the events from 1610 through 1678 to complete your timeline.

 Checking the Catechism
Rose sent her guardian angel to Dona Maria (page 117). Older students should read text paragraphs 328-36 (59-61) in the *CCC*, while younger students review angels in their own catechisms. If desired, complete Activity #43 in *100 Activities*.

📖 **Searching Scripture**
Read Psalm 91 (90):11 and Matthew 18:10, which refer to guardian angels.

Saint Rose of Lima

✏️ Book Summary Test for *Saint Rose of Lima*

Directions: Answer in complete sentences. If necessary, use the back of the page for additional writing space. 100 possible points, 20 points for each answer.

1. In what country did St. Rose live? When did she live?

2. Name at least two saints of the Catholic Church that St. Rose knew.

3. Name at least two miracles attributed to St. Rose after her death.

4. What did St. Rose see as her purpose in life?

5. St. Rose did not hesitate in her obedience to her parents and to her religious superiors. Discuss what role this, as well as her humility, had in her spiritual development. How can you imitate St. Rose of Lima's life?

Saint Rose of Lima,
The Story of the First Canonized Saint of the Americas
Answer Key to Comprehension Questions

Chapters 1 and 2—In Which Rose Is Born, Named, Learns to Read, And Receives the Sacrament of Confirmation
1. The ongoing battle between Rose's mother and grandmother centers on Rose's name. Rose had received in Baptism the name of her grandmother, Isabel, but Rose's mother feels the name "Rose" suits her better due to her resemblance to the flower.
2. Rose was born on the feast day of St. Catherine of Siena.
3. The Flores family moves from Lima to Quivi as it means more money for the family. In addition, it is a welcome relief to move from the city into the mountains.
4. When she receives the Sacrament of Confirmation from Archbishop Turribius, Rose is eleven.

Chapters 3 and 4—In Which Rose Prays and Suffers to Save Souls, and Confides in Doctor John and Dona Maria
1. Rose's "secret" is that she has a great zeal for saving souls—"hundreds and hundreds of souls" (page 27). She offers many prayers and sacrifices so that others may be saved.
2. Doctor John tells Rose of Martin de Porres, who is several years older than Rose and also very interested in the salvation of souls.
3. As the women are prone to gossip and unchristian speech, Rose does not enjoy entertaining many of her mother's guests.

Chapters 5 and 6—In Which Rose Visits the Monasteries of Lima, and Francis Solano Comes to Preach
1. If Rose had been a boy, she would have gone to Santo Domingo to become a priest so she could help the poverty-stricken people of Lima learn about God.
2. On the way to the Monastery of the Incarnation, Rose tells Dona Maria that at the age of five she had consecrated herself to God and His service. Dona Maria tells Rose the story of the founding of the first convent for women in Lima.
3. The powerful message of Francis Solano's sermon is simple charity—loving your neighbor and seeing Christ in all you meet.

Chapters 7 and 8—In Which Don Gonzalo Resolves to Help Rose Become a Poor Clare Nun, and Rose Is Unable to Leave Santo Domingo to Join the Augustinian Convent
1. Rose refers to her statue of the Christ Child as "The Little Doctor."
2. Signs that the saintly bishop Turribius had gone straight to heaven upon his death included a bright cross that was visible in the sky and an eclipse of the moon on the night he died.
3. Although Lima had five different convents for women, Rose hesitated to join any as none of them were Dominican convents.
4. Rose was unable to leave the Dominican church, where she stopped to pray before going to live at the Augustinian convent, as she was miraculously stuck to the floor on her knees before the shrine of Our Lady of the Rosary.

Chapter 9—In Which Rose Becomes a Spouse of Christ
1. Rose took the name "Rose of St. Mary" when she became a Dominican tertiary.
2. It was only in prayer that Rose found relief for her lonely heart.
3. Rose wanted a ring as she heard Christ ask her to become His spouse. The inscription on the ring was to read, "Rose of My Heart, be thou My spouse," Christ's words to her as well as Ferdinand's suggestion for an inscription.

Chapter 10—In Which Rose Builds a Hermitage
1. When Rose's mother does not understand her, Rose prays that God would use this suffering to bring her closer to Him and to help her become a saint.
2. Rose's fasting, hours of prayer, and the giving of her whole life for the saving of souls lead others to compare her to St. Catherine of Siena.
3. Rose spends evenings in her hermitage in prayer rather than recreation or sleep.

Chapter 11—In Which Rose Moves into the Home of Don Gonzalo and then to Her Heavenly Home
1. If she had been a missionary, Rose felt that she would have had a chance to become a martyr for Christ.
2. Although she misses tending her garden and flowers, Rose continues to do needlework and plays her harp, zither, and guitar.
3. Rose of Lima died on the feast of St. Bartholomew (August 24) in 1617.

12 and 13—In Which Peru Pays Its Respects to Rose, and We Learn of Life in Santa Catalina
1. The seven miracles mentioned in these last two chapters include Rose appearing to Alfonsa Serrano after Rose's death; the fragrance of roses and lilies about Rose's dead body; the incident when the pitcher of chocolate came to Rose from Dona Maria; Rose's chain loosening itself after her prayer to the Mother of God; Rose's warm, flexible body hours after death; the unearthly light surrounding the rosary shrine where Rose had prayed; and the cure of the crippled boy.
2. Rose wished to be buried within the cloister of the Dominican Church of Santo Domingo. She was buried in secret due to the crowds that kept coming for relics.
3. Not only was St. Catherine watching over the convent but also it was felt that Rose was aiding Santa Catalina with her prayers, causing an increase in vocations.

Answer Key to Book Summary Test

1. St. Rose lived all of her life in Peru during the late sixteenth and early seventeenth centuries. She was born in 1586 and died on August 24, 1617.
2. St. Rose knew St. Martin de Porres who lived in the same city at the same time as Rose. She received Confirmation from Archbishop Turribius—who is also now a saint. She had attended sermons given by St. Francis Solano in Lima.
3. This book mentions five miracles attributed to St. Rose after her death: Rose appeared to Alfonsa Serrano, as well as others, after her death; there was a fragrance of roses and lilies about Rose's dead body; her body remained warm and flexible hours her after death; an unearthly light surrounded the rosary shrine during the exhibition of Rose's body there; and a crippled boy was cured.
4. St. Rose felt that God had called her to live in the world as a lay person, to pray and suffer for the salvation of souls.
5. Answers will vary.

Study Guide for

Saint Martin de Porres, The Story of the Little Doctor of Lima, Peru

St. Martin de Porres

St. Martin de Porres lived in Lima, Peru—
Loved all kinds of people and animals too.
The color of skin
Did not matter to him;
God created each one, of this he well knew.

He gave to the poor—to all who did need.
His mother's advice he did not always heed.
To his father's he went
Where two years he spent.
His relatives taught him to write and to read.

His sister stayed there while Martin went back
To live with his mother, not in a shack.
From the doctor he learned
While candles he burned.
He prayed and he felt he was slightly off track.

So Martin decided a servant to be.
At fifteen he left for the monastery.
So humble was he
That he couldn't see
Full membership there; they did not agree.

So with black and white habit did they invest
Martin as "brother" despite his protest.
To obey was his goal
No matter the toll.
Virtues abounding he came to possess.

With love earned the favor of men and of mice.
He taught by example of prayer, sacrifice.
He raised from the dead.
Poor people he fed.
Equality for all—it's well worth the price.

Think what you can learn from this saint and his tale.
How you can apply it to help you prevail.
Then mold what you do
And boldly pursue
His pattern of holiness. Follow his trail.

Timeline of Events

Year	Event
1517	Protestant Reformation begins in Europe with Martin Luther
1521	Herman Cortez conquers Aztec empire
1526	Founding of the Mogul Muslim Empire, Kabul (now Afghanistan)
1533	Francisco Pizarro captures the Inca capital, Cuzco and conquers Peru
1534	St. Ignatius of Loyola founds the Society of Jesus
1535	Large silver mines discovered in Peru and Mexico
1543	Copernicus publishes his theory that the earth revolves around the sun
1545-63	First Council of Trent held as called by Pope Paul III
1549	St. Francis Xavier arrives in Japan as a missionary
1551	Founding of the first university in the New World at Lima, Peru
1562	French Wars of Religion begin
1564	Birth of William Shakespeare; death of John Calvin
1567	City of Rio de Janeiro, Argentina, founded
1571	Mediterranean Sea Battle of Lepanto fought; sugar plantations set up in Brazil
1573	Birth of Michelangelo Caravaggio
1575	Plague sweeps through Italy and Sicily
1577	Sir Francis Drake sets out to sail around the world
1579	Birth of St. Martin de Porres
1582	Introduction of the Gregorian Calendar, named for Pope Gregory XIII
1585	Birth of St. John Masias
1586	Birth of St. Rose in Lima, Peru; the Jesuits found missions in Paraguay
1587	Martin leaves Lima to live with his father; death of Mary, Queen of Scots
1588	Defeat of the Spanish Armada
1589	Martin returns to Lima to become an apprentice to a doctor
1590	First microscope made by Hans and Zacharias Janssen
1594	Martin enters the monastery at Santo Domingo
1604	Father Francis Solano preaches famous sermon causing thousands to confess
1605	Publication of *Don Quixote* by Miguel de Cervantes
1606	Australia discovered by the Dutch
1610	First telescope observations made by Galileo
1611	Publication of the King James Bible
1612	Martin raises Brother Thomas from the dead with his prayerful intercession
1617	Death of St. Rose of Lima
1617	Sir Walter Raleigh leads expedition to South American to find El Dorado
1618	Beginning of the Thirty Years' War in Europe
1620	Pilgrims land near Cape Cod
1639	Death of St. Martin de Porres
1642	Birth of Isaac Newton
1645	Death of St. John Masias
1650	Completion of the *Taj Mahal* in Arga, India
1654	Portuguese drive Dutch from Brazil
1678	John Bunyan publishes *Pilgrim's Progress*
1763	Martin de Porres declared venerable; in 1836 Pope Gregory XVI declared him blessed; St. Martin de Porres canonized a saint on May 6, 1962

Saint Martin de Porres

Chapter 1–In Which Martin Shares with a Beggar

 Vocabulary

Senoras who could ride about the city
the *Viceroy('s)* golden carriage

alms
Archbishop

 Comprehension Questions/Narration Prompts
1. What does Jane think would bring her happiness?
2. Martin goes to visit our Lord in the tabernacle to tell him about what sin that he has committed? What commandment did he break?

 Forming Opinions/Drawing Conclusions
Was Martin right to give the coins to the woman? Make a case for the correctness of Martin's action as well as a case for his sinfulness in disobeying his mother. Which is the stronger case? What would you have done?

 For Further Study
Martin lived in Lima, Peru, during the latter half of the sixteenth century. Research the history of Peru and the city of Lima to better understand the political climate, class structure, economics, and general surroundings of Martin. Using your research, write a brief report or prepare an oral presentation.

 Growing in Holiness
Do something to help the poor this week. Donate extra clothing, books, toys, food, or money to a charitable society or to someone you know. Give this week's allowance to a worthy cause or to someone in need that you know personally. Help out at a local soup kitchen or other service agency.

 Geography
Using the map found on page 19 of this study guide, trace the outline of the map as well as the boundary lines of the countries. Label the seas and Amazon River blue. Using the inlay map, note the continent's world position. (Note that this is the same map as completed in the *St. Rose* study guide; do not repeat if you have already copied this map.)

Searching Scripture
Martin was very poor, yet he gave to someone more poor than himself. Read Matthew 19:16-30 on the danger of riches. Compare Martin's gift to the old woman with the widow's mite in Luke 21:1-4.

Chapter 2–In Which Martin and Jane Begin a New Life with Their Father

 Vocabulary
Don Juan de Porres   *soul*

 Comprehension Questions/Narration Prompts
1. Why were Martin and Jane not taught to read and write?
2. Why was Martin sad to see gold bags being loaded onto the Spanish ships?

 Forming Opinions/Drawing Conclusions
Throughout times around the world there has been prejudice between races and/or classes of people. How does Martin feel as a black person with a Spanish father? What appears to be his attitude toward this issue? In reading this book, what have you observed about the race/class situation in Lima during this time?

 Growing in Holiness
On page 11 it states that God had touched Don Juan de Porres' heart and made him feel sorry about the way he had treated his children. Search your heart for your own actions, attitudes, and behavior toward your family members. Speak kind words to each member of your family today and every day.

 Geography
If you have not yet completed your South American map, do so now by labeling the cities of Guayaquil, Ecuador; Lima, Peru; and Callao, Peru. Draw in the Equator and Andes Mountains; label the names of the countries. If you are already familiar with the South American countries, try to label them without use of the map provided.

 Timeline Work
Taping sheets of plain paper end-to-end, make a timeline representing the years from 1517 through 1763. Let three inches equal 25 years. Mark on your timeline the dates and events from 1517 through 1579, using information from page 18 of this study guide.

Searching Scripture
Watching the laborers loading the Spanish ships with gold, Martin was sad. Read what Scripture says about true riches in Matthew 6:19-21 and 6:24-34, and in Psalm 49 (48): 17-21.

Chapter 3–In Which Martin Returns to Lima to Become a Doctor

 Vocabulary

start to learn a *trade*   *hear mass*
Dr. de Rivero's *apprentice*   *priest*

 Comprehension Questions/Narration Prompts
1. Why did Martin return to his mother? Why did Jane stay with her father?
2. What is Martin's dream?
3. What does Martin feel was God's Will for those who lived on earth?

 Forming Opinions/Drawing Conclusions
Explain how Martin's mother's feelings for him had changed in the last two years. What were some of the causes of this change?

 For Further Study
Martin's father was appointed Governor of Panama. Panama is a country about the size of Maine. Locate Panama on a map. How far north of Guayaquil, Ecuador, is it? Spain colonized Panama less than one hundred years before Juan de Porres was appointed governor. Gold, silver, pearls, and emeralds in great quantities were shipped to Spain from Panama. Research the country of Panama, paying special attention to the time period of the sixteenth century.

 Growing in Holiness
"All that would matter in Heaven would be how well one had done his duty on earth" (page 22). Consider how well you do your duty. Resolve to do each chore or assignment cheerfully and willingly knowing that God's Will for you each day is to fulfill your duty as student, brother/sister, child to your parents, and friend to all.

✓ **Checking the Catechism**
Martin went to "hear mass" each morning. Younger students can learn more about the Mass by studying this topic in their catechisms. Older students may study the "Sacramental Sacrifice" in the *Catechism of the Catholic Church* (*CCC*) text paragraphs 1356-1381 (271-286). If desired, complete Activity #12 and/or Activity #52 in *100 Activities Based on the Catechism of the Catholic Church* (*100 Activities*).

 Searching Scripture
Martin states that he loves God by loving others. Read Matthew 10:40, Matthew 25:40, and John 15:12.

Chapter 4–In Which Martin Grows in Grace

 Vocabulary

given Himself to *ransom* mankind
had been long deep in *slumber*

brother
Dominican

 Comprehension Questions/Narration Prompts
1. Why does Martin need so many candles?
2. What are Martin's goals in the monastery?
3. Why does Martin go to Santo Domingo only as a helper?

 Forming Opinions/Drawing Conclusions
Explain how "candles in the dark" helped lead Martin into a new way of life.

 For Further Study
Martin devoted much time to mediating upon the crucifix and the sufferings of Jesus—"Why was it like this?" "Why did you do so much?" (page 30). Research the devotion of the Way of the Cross, which is also known as the Stations of the Cross. When did this devotion originate? What religious order helped make it popular? By what other names is it known?

✞ **Growing in Holiness**
Martin knows that he wanted to spend his whole life helping people to understand how much God loves them. By spending much time praying in front of the crucifix, he comes to realize the depth of God's love for each of us. Memorize the indulgenced prayer below. Pray this prayer often before a crucifix. You too can light candles and let Jesus help you understand the little things you can do each day to show God's love to others.

Prayer before a Crucifix (for younger students)

> Look down on me, good and gentle Jesus, while I kneel here. Make my soul strong in faith, hope, and love. Make me really sorry for all my sins so I will never sin again. I am sad when I see the wounds on Your hands and feet, and think of the words of Your prophet, David: "They have pierced my hands and my feet." Lord Jesus Crucified, have mercy on us! Amen.

 Searching Scripture
Martin stated that God has great need of people to do small things for Him. Read Matthew 18:1-4 on becoming as little children. Find where in the Bible it states that those who are last will be first. (This is found in the Bible at least four times; see how many you can find.)

Chapter 5–In Which Martin Settles into the Convent of Santo Domingo

 Vocabulary

the *volume* he was reading
was often the case with *invalids*

scapular
rule

 Comprehension Questions/Narration Prompts
1. What was Martin's first job at the convent? What value did he place on obedience?
2. Name two other jobs Martin later had at Santo Domingo.

 Forming Opinions/Drawing Conclusions
1. Do you think Brother James is the same race as Martin? Explain your answer.
2. This chapter ends with Martin hoping to help Father Peter, "Maybe something can be done" (page 45). Describe what might happen between Martin and Father Peter in their next encounter. How do you think Martin will help Father Peter? (After reading the next chapter, be sure to compare your prediction with what actually happens.)

 For Further Study
When Martin moves into the monastery, he starts to wear the religious habit of the Dominicans of Santo Domingo, with the exception of the scapular. Using a Catholic encyclopedia or dictionary, research the scapular—which literally means "shoulder cloak"—and symbolizes the yoke of Christ. Find the two popular meanings of this word. Be sure to also research the Sabbatine Privilege, which is sometimes called the Scapular Promise. Present your research in a short report. (Many children are invested in the brown scapular of our Lady of Mount Carmel around the time of First Communion. If you were invested and have gotten out of the habit of wearing your scapular, begin again to wear it daily.)

 Growing in Holiness
Martin states, "I must not be afraid of what people think of me, or the cross things they say" (page 40). Imitate Martin's obedience and humility. Do not defend yourself even when you know you are right. Do what is right without regard to what others may say or think. Do not be upset or angry when others are cross. Offer these sacrifices to God.

✓ **Checking the Catechism**
Older students may read text paragraphs 224, 1328, and 2637-38 in the *CCC* (43, 547, 550, and 555). If desired, complete Activity #66 in *100 Activities*, "Giving Thanks: Counting Your Blessings."

 Searching Scripture
Pray Psalm 111 (110), Psalm 136 (135):1-9, and Psalm 148 to give God thanks and praise.

Chapter 6–In Which Martin Performs His Religious Duties

 Vocabulary

vegetables for the *brethren* *sacristan*
beckoned to the little creature *vestments*

 Comprehension Questions/Narration Prompts
1. After Mass, Martin wants to do one thing but did another. What are these two things?
2. Why does Martin feel responsible for the ragged linens found by Brother Michael?

Forming Opinions/Drawing Conclusions
Why is the Holy Eucharist the "best medicine"?

 For Further Study
Martin speaks of Brother Michael, who was the sacristan in charge of the vestments, altar candles, and altar cloths. Research the various vestments the priests wear at Mass—amice, alb, cincture, maniple, stole and chasuble—as well as the order they are put on. One altar cloth, always made of linen, is required by the rubrics of the Mass to cover the altar during Mass. (The new order of the Mass changed the requirements from three altar clothes to one.) Other altar cloths include the corporal, purificator, pall, and burse as well as the different types of veils—tabernacle, chalice, humeral, and ciborium. Prepare an outline to summarize your research.

Growing in Holiness
Each morning Martin praises Jesus on the crucifix, and then says a prayer to the Blessed Mother and St. Joseph, as well as the patron saint of the Dominicans, St. Dominic. Each morning begin your day with Martin's prayer to Jesus, "Praised be Jesus Christ!" as well as a brief aspiration to Mary, Joseph, and your patron saint. Remember too Martin's attitude toward each new day: "Another day was about to begin, another collection of hours in which to love God and serve those about him" (page 47).

 Timeline Work
Add the events from 1582 through 1611 to your timeline.

 Searching Scripture
Read Psalm 63 (62):1-9 and Psalm 84 (83):1-4. Memorize one of these Psalm passages. Use it as a thanksgiving prayer after Communion.

Chapter 7–In Which Martin Rests from His Religious Duties

 Vocabulary

The *latter* had run all the way   *altar linens*
as he had been *bidden*   *Tertiary*

 Comprehension Questions/Narration Prompts
1. What is Martin's idea to help save the convent's pictures and raise money?
2. What does Father Prior say is one thing that money can't buy?
3. What is the main lesson that Martin teaches the children of Limatambo?

 Forming Opinions/Drawing Conclusions
1. Martin takes several weeks and teaches the children the catechism. Which part of the catechism would you consider to be the most important to teach to others?
2. Martin retells the "thrilling stories of the Gospel" (page 64). Pick two or three stories from the Gospels that you could tell to younger children. Explain why you chose these particular stories and the lessons they teach. Remember that a story from the Gospel would have to come from one of the following books of the Bible: Matthew, Mark, Luke or John. Chose too one story from the Old Testament.

 Growing in Holiness
Sanctifying grace is the means God uses to live in each of us who keep our hearts pure for Him. It is our participation in the divine life and God's presence within us. Remember not to look at the outside appearance of a person but to look for a sign of God's presence within each person you meet. Do not be put off by any person's color or physical appearance. Mother Teresa of Calcutta believed that Jesus comes to us in many disguises—sometimes distressing disguises. Look carefully for Him each day.

✓ **Checking the Catechism**
The word "catechism" comes from the Greek word *katechein*, which means "to instruct verbally." Most catechisms are in question/answer form. The Baltimore Catechism, which was for many years the standard catechism, was first published in the United States in 1885. In 1985 the Roman Synod recommended that a universal Catechism be prepared for the Church. Read the "Apostolic Constitution *Fidei Depositum* on the Publication of the Catechism of the Catholic Church" found in the introductory materials of the *Catechism of the Catholic Church*.

 Searching Scripture
"How much better it was to give than to receive!" (page 58) Read what the Bible teaches regarding this thought in Sirach 4:31 (Ecclesiasticus 4:36) and Acts 20:35.

Chapter 8–In Which Martin Becomes a Dominican Brother

Vocabulary
make a *solemn* promise
My good *mistress* is sick

lay brother
First Order of Saint Dominic

Comprehension Questions/Narration Prompts
1. Why does Martin resist becoming a lay brother? Why does he then agree to it?
2. What does Martin say is one of the "most wonderful things a person can hope for in this world"?
3. What miracle occurs when Martin feeds the beggars?

Forming Opinions/Drawing Conclusions
Discuss Martin's attitude toward giving God credit for his gifts. How does this fit in with being proud of your accomplishments?

For Further Study
Martin understood animals, and they seem to have understood him. Research another saint of the Catholic Church who was very dedicated to animals—St. Francis of Assisi. Write a short report on this saint. Be sure to include his "Canticle of the Sun," which is a poem in praise of all God's creation.

Growing in Holiness
Re-read the last paragraph on page 67 (and carried over to page 68) regarding Martin's thoughts on work. Proverbs 14:23 relates labor to abundance or profit. Work this week with a renewed sense that you are doing God's work. Enjoy the "blessedness of work." Work without complaining—with no expectation of reward except from your heavenly Father. Use short aspirations throughout the day to rededicate your work to God.

Checking the Catechism
"Only people in the state of Sanctifying Grace can love their neighbor the way God wants" (page 73). Younger students should study the two great commandments in their catechism while older students research this topic in the *CCC*. If desired, complete Activity #19 from *100 Activities*.

Searching Scripture
Read the two separate accounts regarding the multiplication of the loaves as found in Matthew 14:13-21 (Mark 6:34-44 and Luke 9:10-17) and Matthew 15:32-38 (Mark 8:1-9).

Chapter 9—In Which We Meet Martin's Saintly Friends

Vocabulary
they must have a *dowry*
Before them *loomed* the tower
ordained
Last Sacraments

Comprehension Questions/Narration Prompts
1. What does Martin's heart make him ask Brother John about?
2. Why does Martin say that the dead are happy?
3. Who is La Rosita?

Growing in Holiness
Martin and his friend John had a special greeting. One would say, "Praised be Jesus Christ." The other would reply, "For ever and forever. Amen" (page 75). Use this greeting or one of your own choosing to greet your brothers and sisters, and your friends. Remember that holy friends help each other to attain heaven. Do not be afraid to be holy and speak about Jesus to others. Memorize Matthew 10:32-33 on admitting knowledge of Jesus to others and the punishment for those who deny Him.

✓ Checking the Catechism
Works of mercy are defined in the *CCC* (text paragraph 2447) as "charitable actions by which we come to the aid of our neighbor in his spiritual and bodily necessities." Review the chart on page 34 of this study guide. Determine whether the works of mercy are corporal (dealing with the body) or spiritual (dealing with the soul). Place a "C" or "S" to the right of each work to indicate this designation. Complete the chart as you read through the story of Martin's life, adding his actions under each appropriate category. For example, in Chapter 5, we find the following: admonish the sinner and bear wrongs patiently. In Chapter 6, note these: forgive all injuries, and pray for the living and the dead. We can add these from Chapter 7: feed the hungry, and instruct the ignorant. Continue to add to this list, noting Martin's specific action and citing the page number until you have at least one citation for each of these fourteen works of mercy. (There are more than one incident for many of these works.) Going back to Chapters 5 through 7, record the specific actions of Martin for each chapter in the appropriate place on the chart. Cite the page numbers for each event. Add Martin's actions of visiting the sick and comforting the sorrowful from this chapter.

Searching Scripture
Martin and Rose were both baptized in the same church, San Sebastian. Read the following Scripture passages: Romans 6:1-11 and Matthew 28:19 on Baptism. Read too Matthew 25:31-46 regarding the actions upon which we will be judged.

Chapter 10–In Which Martin Performs Several Miracles

 Vocabulary

a black and white *clad* figure *convent*
in the *Moorish* city of Algiers *novice*

 Comprehension Questions/Narration Prompts
1. How does Martin know Anthony will come to see him? What does Martin leave for him?
2. Name three special gifts or powers that God grants to Martin.

 Forming Opinions/Drawing Conclusions
1. Why does Martin not wish to tell Prior what happened with Brother Thomas?
2. Discuss why God would give gifts like levitation, bilocation, and the gift of healing—even raising others from the dead—to Martin. What virtue would be necessary before God would be likely to bestow such gifts and powers?

 For Further Study
Martin purchases not one but several *mantillas* for his niece. Some years ago all women wore these in church. Research the Church's practices on head coverings for women. Read 1 Corinthians 11:1-16. Read the article on www.ewtn.com. Go to "Faith" at the top of the home page, then click on "Catholic Q&A," then to "Faith FAQs," then to "General Questions," and then "Head Covering in Church." Write a short essay supporting this practice or refuting it. Be sure to use quotations and facts to support your opinion. (Note: For those girls who might be interested, *mantillas* and chapel caps can be purchased from many Catholic suppliers.)

 Growing in Holiness
All of the brothers and priests at the convent of Santo Domingo have kind words to say about Brother Martin. Be sure to speak only kind words this week about those who live with you. Remember that love is patient and kind. (See 1 Corinthians 13:4.)

✓ **Checking the Catechism**
Add the following to the chart on the works of mercy: bury the dead (requested to do so), shelter the homeless, visit the imprisoned, clothe the naked, and give drink to the thirsty. Be sure to cite the page numbers from this chapter for each event.

 Searching Scripture
Anthony returns the morning of his mother's cure to thank Martin. Read Luke 17:11-19 about ten lepers whom Jesus cured—only one returned to thank Jesus.

Chapter 11–In Which Martin Shows His Wisdom and Spiritual Gifts

 Vocabulary

made . . . Lima *resound* to his . . . sermons   *chapel*
redeemed by the Precious Blood   *Holy Faith*

 Comprehension Questions/Narration Prompts
1. What does Martin say is the most important thing in life?
2. What incident shows that Martin was able to "read people's souls"?

Forming Opinions/Drawing Conclusions
1. St. Turribius of Lima was the archbishop there from 1581-1606. He is credited with baptizing and confirming nearly one million souls. He preached that "time is not our own and we must give a strict accounting of it." Knowing this, what should you do differently? What habits should you cultivate? Which habits must you break?
2. Martin had only two years of formal schooling yet was considered wise and holy. "The school of Christ is the school of charity. In the last day, when the general examination takes place, there will be no question at all on the text of Aristotle . . . or the paragraphs of Justinian. Charity will be the whole syllabus." –St. Robert Bellarmine (Aristotle was a fourth-century BC Greek influential philosopher. Justinian was a sixth-century Roman emperor who gathered all the Roman laws into one code.) How does the life of Martin illustrate this maxim? What knowledge is important for sanctity and eternal happiness?
3. Why do you think St. Martin de Porres was named the patron saint of social justice and inter-racial relations? Support your answer with incidents from his life.

 Growing in Holiness
The young novice who took the coin acted as though he had acted in secret. Read Luke 12:2-3 regarding "secrets." Jesus says that what is hidden will be revealed, and what has been whispered will be proclaimed from the housetops. You are never alone. God is All-present, All-knowing. Whisper your love to Him often this week, and increase your awareness of His constant loving presence. Mediate on Psalm 139 (138):1-18.

 Checking the Catechism
Brother Ferdinand states that Martin knew the Bible well enough to quote it extensively. Older students should read text paragraphs 120-33, "The Canon of Scripture" in the *CCC* (17-24). See how quickly you can find all of the Bible verses listed in Activity #26 of *100 Activities*. Younger students may reference their own catechisms on the topic of the Bible.

 Searching Scripture
Martin, with little formal schooling, counseled many more learned men. (Complete your chart with Martin's counsel of the doubtful.) Read Luke 10:21. Martin always offered words of encouragement to everyone at Santo Domingo. Read Hebrews 3:13.

Chapter 12–In Which Martin Begins the Only Life that Matters

 Vocabulary

a famous *scholar* *miracle*
hovels of the poor *Nicene Creed*

 Comprehension Questions/Narration Prompts
1. What does Martin predict about his death and how does he present it?
2. What does Martin say about our life on earth? What does he say is "the only life that matters"?
3. Why does the Viceroy decide to wait before seeing the dying Martin?
4. What prayer does Martin hear just before he dies?

 Forming Opinions/Drawing Conclusions
1. Many saints did not consider themselves worthy of the priesthood—St. Francis of Assisi for example. Martin de Porres did not even consider himself worthy to become a Dominican brother. Discuss this attitude in relation to today's emphasis on competitiveness, finishing first, and being the best that you can be.
2. What virtues do Martin display when he proclaims that the miracles that happen at his hands are the work of God, in answer to a simple prayer?

 Growing in Holiness
Martin reveals that upon the hour of his death the devil tried to make him afraid of death. "But he still could hope in God's mercy" (page 109). Remember that God is always more willing to be merciful than just. Do not fall into the sin of despair, but be willing to ask God for His forgiveness and His mercy. Share this thought with at least one other person within the next week. (See answer key for pertinent Scripture quotations.)

✓ **Checking the Catechism**
Martin hears the words of the creed upon his deathbed. Younger students should study the Nicene Creed in their catechisms. This creed should be memorized by all students. Older students can read text paragraphs 185-87, 195, 242, 245, and 465 in the *CCC* (33-35). If desired, complete Activity #34 and/or Activity #74 in *100 Activities*.

📖 **Searching Scripture**
Although Martin has no fear of death, and in fact embraces it, the devil still tempted him. But he relies on the mercy of God. Read Psalm 71 (70) and Psalm 131 (130). Imagine St. Martin quietly holding his crucifix, and reciting these passages as he lies near death.

Saint Martin de Porres   33

Chapter 13—In Which Martin, a True Friend of Lima, Is Buried

Vocabulary
The sorrow which had *prevailed* all night   medals
be *pallbearers* at a poor Negro's funeral   *Prior*

Comprehension Questions/Narration Prompts
1. Why does Father Cyprian want a miracle to attribute to the intercession of the deceased Martin?
2. What is Dona Catherine's prayer as she asks Martin's help in obtaining a cure for her withered arm?
3. When and where does St. Martin de Porres die?

Forming Opinions/Drawing Conclusions
Explain the symbolism of the name of this chapter, "Hero in Black and White."

For Further Study
Martin's pallbearers include a bishop and an archbishop. Research some officials of the Catholic Church. In your research include such positions as pope, prelates, bishop, archbishop, cardinal, vicar general, and monsignor. Use references such as a Catholic dictionary or encyclopedia, the Code of Canon Law, a secular encyclopedia, or the Internet. Write a short report, or construct a chart diagramming this information.

✝ Growing in Holiness
After completing the exercises below, recite a prayer of praise to God using some of the ideas found in the Psalms. Use this prayer to praise God every day this week. You may wish to include a prayer of thanksgiving for the example set by His saint, Martin de Porres.

Timeline Work
Add the events from 1612 through 1763 to complete your timeline.

✓ Checking the Catechism
Upon the healing of Dona Catherine's arm, Dona Jacoba and Dona Catherine praise God. Many of the Psalms are prayers of praise to God. Older students may read text paragraphs 2585-97 in the *CCC* (243 and 540). If desired, complete Activity #67 in *100 Activities*, "Praying the Psalms," to become familiar with some of the Psalms.

📖 Searching Scripture
Search the Bible for Psalms that praise God. Memorize several passages of these Psalms and begin to pray them regularly.

Martin's Works of Mercy

Nature of Work	C/S	Martin's Action	Page No.
Feed the Hungry			
Instruct the Ignorant			
Clothe the Naked			
Admonish the Sinner			
Bear Wrongs Patiently			
Visit the Sick			
Bury the Dead			
Shelter the Homeless			
Comfort the Sorrowful			
Counsel the Doubtful			
Give Drink to the Thirsty			
Visit the Imprisoned			
Forgive all Injuries			
Pray for the Living and the Dead			

Book Summary Test for *Saint Martin de Porres*

Directions: Answer in complete sentences. If necessary, use the back of the page for additional writing space. 100 possible points, 20 points for each answer.

1. In what centuries did St. Martin de Porres live? In what city and country did he spend almost all of his life?

2. Describe Martin's family life.

3. In what profession did Martin receive training beginning at the age of ten? At what age did Martin move to the Santo Domingo monastery and in what capacity? How long was he there?

4. Name at least two miracles attributed to Martin's intercession before his death. What were the two miracles attributed to his intercession immediately after his death?

5. Name two of Martin's contemporaries in Lima who also became saints. What can you do to help your friends become saints?

Saint Martin de Porres, The Story of the Little Doctor of Lima, Peru
Answer Key to Comprehension Questions

Chapter 1—In Which Martin Shares with a Beggar
1. Jane thinks that clothes, a nice house, and a father who cared for her will bring her happiness.
2. Martin goes to Jesus to tell him that he has disobeyed his mother, which the fourth commandment forbids.

Chapter 2—In Which Martin and Jane Begin a New Life with Their Father
1. Martin and Jane were not taught to read and write, because they were black children from a poor mother. No schools were available to them.
2. The bags of gold made Martin sad as he knew that the Spaniards often mistreated the workers. He knew that many workers had died in the mines in order to obtain these riches for other people.

Chapter 3—In Which Martin Returns to Lima to Become a Doctor
1. Martin returned to his mother in Lima to help her. Jane stayed with her father in Guayaquil to continue her training into a capable woman and wife.
2. Martin has a dream to be a doctor and make sick people well.
3. Martin feels that God's Will for us is to love one another. Inside each of us is a soul that is the image of God Himself. We must look for this in each other.

Chapter 4—In Which Martin Grows in Grace
1. Martin needs candles as he spent his nights and evenings on his knees praying in front of his crucifix.
2. Martin wishes to help people who are tired, sick and unhappy—and to let them know how much God loves them.
3. Martin wishes to be only a servant at Santo Domingo as he does not wish to be important but to do little things for God.

Searching Scripture
"The last shall be first": Matthew 19:30, Matthew 20:16, Mark 10:31, and Luke 13:30.

Chapter 5—In Which Martin Settles into the Convent of Santo Domingo
1. Martin's first job at Santo Domingo is as a barber. He shows that he prized obedience over the respect and love his fellow man have for him.
2. Martin later had charge of the clothes room at the monastery as well as care of the sick (page 42).

Chapter 6—In Which Martin Performs His Religious Duties
1. After Mass, Martin wants to stay and pray, but instead he leaves to do his work—sweep the halls, work in the kitchen, rake and weed the garden, and feed the sick.
2. Martin took it upon himself to feed the dogs and cats that wandered into the monastery, but he had never thought to feed the mice and rats who had eaten the linens.

Chapter 7—In Which Martin Rests from His Religious Duties
1. Martin has the idea of selling himself as a slave to pay off the debt of the convent.
2. Father Prior tells Martin that one thing that money cannot buy is a faithful heart—like Martin's.
3. Martin teaches the children of Limatambo that God loves us all—no matter what our color—and that as long as our souls are clean, we are never alone as God is living in our hearts (page 64).

Chapter 8—In Which Martin Becomes a Dominican Brother
1. Martin does not think he is worthy to become a lay brother. He later agrees to become one out of obedience to Father Prior.
2. "To work, when that work is offered to God in union with the merits of Christ, is one of the most wonderful things a person can hope for in this world" (page 68).
3. When Martin feeds the beggars, the basket from which he is passing out food never empties.

Chapter 9—In Which We Meet Martin's Saintly Friends
1. Martin is concerned about the homeless that are within the city of Lima, but the girl orphans are especially dear to his heart.
2. Martin states that the dead are happy because they have begun the only life that matters.
3. La Rosita is the girl who later would be known as St. Rose of Lima.

Chapter 10—In Which Martin Performs Several Miracles
1. Martin knows that Anthony will come to see him as he knows Anthony wants to tell him that his mother has gotten better. Martin leaves Anthony a new pair of shoes.
2. God grants Martin the gifts of miraculous travel (ubiquity), levitation, and the ability to raise men from the dead.

Chapter 11—In Which Martin Shows His Wisdom and Spiritual Gifts
1. Martin states that the most important thing in life is this: "to think about You a lot, to come to know how good You are, and then to love You more than anyone or anything" (page 93).
2. Martin shows that he could "read people's souls" when he confronts the boy who took the coin from his room, even though Martin was not in the room when the coin was taken.

Chapter 12—In Which Martin Begins the Only Life that Matters
1. Martin predicts his death four days before it occurs. He wears a new habit as he states that he wishes to have one for his burial.
2. Martin tells us that this life is unimportant, and our eternal life is the only life that matters.
3. Martin was communicating with St. Dominic and the Blessed Mother. The Viceroy feels that that they are certainly more important than he. So he waits to see Martin until Martin agrees to see him (after his heavenly visitors have left).
4. The last prayer that Martin hears before his death was the Nicene Creed.

Growing in Holiness
Psalm 103 (102):8-10, Psalm 130 (129), and Psalm 136 (135) are some of the Psalm passages that refer to God's mercy.

Chapter 13—In Which Martin, a True Friend of Lima, Is Buried
1. Father Cyprian wants a miracle to prove that Martin has attained heaven and to strengthen the faith of Martin's friends.
2. Dona Catherine prays for faith and the greater glory of God.
3. St. Martin de Porres died on November 5, 1639, in Lima, Peru.

Answer Key to Book Summary Test

1. Martin de Porres lived in the sixteenth and seventeenth centuries (1579-1639) in Lima, Peru.
2. Martin was the illegitimate child of a white Spanish nobleman and a black Panamanian. His mother was very poor and tried to support herself, Martin, and his sister by taking in laundry. His father was absent from the home until Martin reached the age of eight. Martin lived with his father for two years before becoming apprenticed to a doctor in Lima at which time he rented a room and lived on his own. At the age of fifteen, Martin entered the Dominican monastery of Santo Domingo in Lima as a servant.
3. Beginning at the age of ten, Martin received medical training and later used this training at the monastery to care for his fellow Dominicans as well as the poor. At the age of fifteen, he

Saint Martin de Porres

joined the Dominican monastery in Lima, Peru, as a servant, and later quite unwillingly became a lay brother. While at the monastery, he tended the herb garden, using herbs for medicine. He moved into the Holy Rosary Convent at the age of fifteen and remained there until his death at the age of sixty.

4. Miracles attributed to Martin before his death include the multiplication of food as he distributed it to the poor, the peaceful removal of the rats from the monastery, the speedy transportation of Martin and his companions from the picnic, the subsiding of the waters of the Rimac River, and the restoration of life to Brother Thomas due to Martin's prayers. In addition, he is reported to have had various miraculous powers: bilocation, (being two places at once) passing through locked doors, and levitation (rising above the ground) as he prayed before a crucifix. Immediately after his death, prayers to him resulted in the cure of a woman with a withered arm. At his funeral, his body became full of color, flexible, and warm.
5. Rose of Lima, John Masias, and Archbishop Turribius were all contemporaries of Martin de Porres. Answers to the second part of this question will vary.

Study Guide for

*King David and His Songs,
A Story of the Psalms*

King David

Young David, a shepherd, his father's last son,
Killed the Philistine giant—the battle was won.
With slingshot and stone,
His name became known.
Bravery acclaimed, David's fame had begun.

Anointed by Samuel as a young man,
Next in line to the throne was the secret plan.
With Saul out of sorts,
David went to his courts—
With song cheered the king as music often can.

Friends became David and Jonathan, Saul's son.
But Saul's hatred of David had by then begun.
He was forced to flee,
Despite Jonathan's plea.
David lived as an outlaw—a man on the run.

In battle died Jonathan and his father Saul,
And David as king did Judah install.
Wise, humble, and strong,
David still sang His song.
God blessed him with power; his kingdom did sprawl.

He won many battles, was kind, just, and true.
King of Judah and Israel—united the two.
Thirty years as king reigned,
Jerusalem obtained,
Brought the Ark of the Covenant to Jerusalem too.

With a strong faith in God, still David did sin.
Each time he'd repent—accept God's discipline.
We remember his songs,
Instead of his wrongs.
His psalms we recite, and feel peace within.

Think what you can learn from this saint and his tale.
How you can apply it to help you prevail.
Then mold what you do
And boldly pursue
His pattern of holiness. Follow his trail.

Timeline of Events

Year	Event
1200	Iron begins to be used by the Hittites in the Near East; period of the Judges (1200-1020); 20th Dynasty of Egypt (to 1090); decline of Egypt begins
1193	Destruction of Troy during the Trojan War
1190	21st Dynasty of Egypt (to 945); civil war begins under Ramses XI
1146	Nebuchodonosor (Nebuchadnezzar) I, king of Babylon (to 1123)
1040	Samuel, the last of the judges, anoints Saul as the first king of the Israelites
1030	Birth of David, eighth son of Isai (Jesse) of Bethlehem
1116	Tiglath-pileser (to 1077) founds Assyrian Empire; conquers Babylon
1000	Death of Samuel; King Saul killed in battle; King David crowned King of Juda(h)
1000-900	Iron tools are made in India; Phoenicians begin use of alphabet; Greeks establish colonies in the Aegean Islands; earliest use of iron in Greece; beginning of Hebrew alphabet and Hebrew literature; water supply system through reinforced subterranean tunnels built in Jerusalem; Indian lunar year has 360 days adjusted at random to coincide with solar year
994	King David captures Jerusalem and makes it his capital; returns Ark of the Covenant and tablets of Ten Commandments to Jerusalem
993	King David crowned King of Israel
961	Death of King David; succeeded by his son Solomon who developed trade, enacted laws, and imposed taxes
957	Beginning of the construction of the Temple, the fourth year of King Solomon's reign
950	Dedication of the Temple in Jerusalem as built by King Solomon with help from King Hiram of Tyre, (969-936)
945	22nd Dynasty of Egypt (to 745) begins with Sheshonk I (to 920)
935	Revival of Assyria
922	Death of Solomon under whose reign Israel reaches height of its civilization; kingdom split between two of Solomon's sons—Juda(h) in the south, under Roboam (Rehoboam) - 922-915, and Israel in the north, under Jeroboam - 922-901
879	Samaria (formerly Sichem) rebuilt as capital of Israel, destroyed by Sargon II in 722
813	Carthage founded as trading center with Tyre

Note: All dates are BC (BCE). Because of the limitations of recorded early history, all dates are approximate. Current historians, influenced by Assyrian inscriptions, have now placed David's birth and reign thirty to fifty years later than the dates previously accepted. Expect some date variations from source to source.

King David and His Songs 43

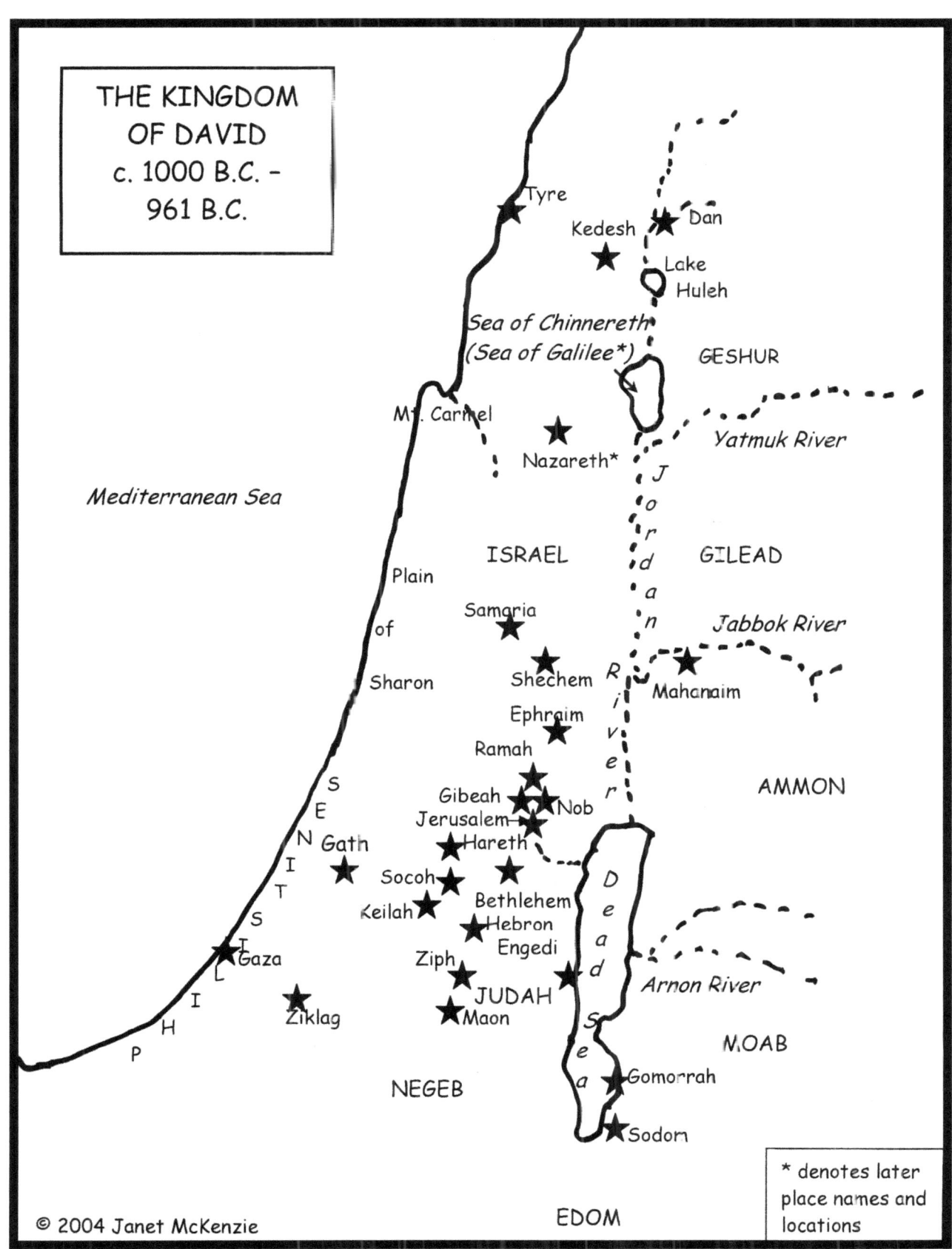

Chapters 1 through 3–In Which Samuel Anoints David

⟶Vocabulary
a sacrifice of *jubilation*   *merit*

Comprehension Questions/Narration Prompts
1. How many sons did Isai (Jesse) have? Where did David fit into the family?
2. What did Samuel do when he met David?
3. What was David's favorite pastime?
4. Why did David go to King Saul?

Forming Opinions/Drawing Conclusions
1. Why do you suppose that Samuel anointed Isai's (Jesse's) youngest son David? Why did Samuel insist that this anointing be kept secret?
2. Explain the friendship between David and Jonathan.
3. Discuss the reaction of David's brothers to his offer to fight against Goliath.

✠ Growing in Holiness
David was able to assess his Godly gifts and to use these gifts in the service of God. Devise two practical ways that you can use your Godly gifts for His service. Remember that these abilities are gifts; all credit for them always must be given to God.

Timeline Work
Taping sheets of plain paper end-to-end, make a timeline representing the years from BC 1200 to BC 813. Let three inches equal 25 years. Mark on your timeline the dates and events from BC 1200 through BC 1116 as found on page 42 of this study guide.

✓ Checking the Catechism
Older students may read about anointing in text paragraphs 436, 695, 786, and 1293-1296 (82, 139, 266-267, 318, and 328) of the *CCC*. Younger students may review anointing in the Sacraments of Baptism, Confirmation, Anointing of the Sick, and Holy Orders.

Searching Scripture
1. Read 1 Samuel (1 Kings) 16:1-23 on Samuel's anointing of David and David's entrance into Saul's service as musician and armor-bearer.
2. Note the discrepancy in the Psalms' numbering between the Douay-Rheims and New American translations. (See page xiii of the Tan biography.) If desired, read the New American translation of the Psalms from these chapters: Psalms 23, 8, and 27.
3. Read about Jesus' anointing at Bethany in Matthew 26:6-13.

Chapters 4 through 6–In Which David Kills the Philistine Goliath, and Saul Grows Envious of David

Vocabulary
watched with *bated* breath
terrible fits of *melancholy*
temple
mercy

Comprehension Questions/Narration Prompts
1. To whom did David give credit for his victory over Goliath?
2. Immediately after David's victory over Goliath, how did Saul feel toward David? How did his feelings change as time went on?
3. How did Saul endanger David's life? What did Jonathan do to help David?

Forming Opinions/Drawing Conclusions
1. Retell the story of the battle between David and Goliath, comparing their weapons.
2. Imagine how Jonathan felt as he watched tensions grow between his father and his best friend. Can you think of anything Jonathon could have done to help establish peace between the two?

✝ Growing in Holiness
Although physically strong, David possessed the virtue of meekness. When confronted with Saul's angry accusations, he tries to soothe Saul, and then merely walks away. Imitate this meekness when you are confronted. Do not confuse meekness with weakness.

Geography
Trace the map of the Kingdom of David from page 43 of this study guide. (Note that geographical names have been converted on the map to the names used in the New American translation of the Bible. When listed, the terms as used in the Windeatt biography are listed first with the New American terms in parentheses. See "Note on Personal and Geographical Names" on page 60 of this study guide.) Label and color blue the three seas, four rivers, and one lake. Label too the following cities: Bethlehem, Saul's home of Gabaa (Gibeah), and Socho (Socoh) where David fought Goliath (Vale of the Terebinth).

✓ Checking the Catechism
Older students may read the teachings the *CCC* on meekness and gentleness in text paragraphs 716, 736, 1716, 1832, and 2219 (359-362 and 390). Younger students may read about the Beatitudes and the fruits of the Holy Spirit in their catechisms.

Searching Scripture
1. Read 1 Samuel (1 Kings) 17:1-19:10 on Goliath's death and Saul's growing hatred of David.
2. If desired, read the New American translation of Psalms 138, 70, and 15.

Chapters 7 and 8–In Which David Escapes King Saul and Lives as a Fugitive

 Vocabulary
wrath of his own *sovereign*   *consecrated*

 Comprehension Questions/Narration Prompts
1. How did David escape from King Saul?
2. Why did David feel uneasy after he left Achimelech (Ahimelech), the high priest?
3. How did David escape from the Philistines after allowing himself to be captured?
4. Name some places that David lived after escaping the Philistines.

 Forming Opinions/Drawing Conclusions
Discuss whether the following actions of David were wise choices: his escape from Saul through the window, his dishonesty with the high priest, his turning to the Philistines, and his pretense of madness in escaping the Philistines. What might some future consequences of these choices be?

 Growing in Holiness
"From earliest boyhood David had turned to God in time of trouble, relying upon His strength instead of his own for a solution to all difficulties" (page 38). ". . . he had immediate recourse to prayer" (page 47). Use prayer as a frontline remedy rather than a last recourse. Note what happened to David when he did not listen to his heart when it called him to prayer (page 38).

 Geography
Locate and label the following place names on the map started in the previous lesson: Ramatha (Ramah), Nobe (Nob), Gath (in the land of the Philistines), Moab, Haret (Hereth), Ceila (Keilah), and Ziph.

✓ **Checking the Catechism**
Older students may read about David and the Psalms in text paragraphs 304, 1093, 1156, 1177, 2578-80, 2585-89, 2596-97, 2641, and 2657 (8, 243, and 540) of the *CCC*. Younger students may review their catechisms references to using Scripture and the Psalms in prayer.

📖 **Searching Scripture**
1. Read 1 Samuel (1 Kings) 19:11-23:24 in Sacred Scripture. This passage relates David's meetings with Samuel, Jonathan, and Achimelech (Ahimelech), his capture by the Philistines, and his battle at Ceila (Keilah).
2. If desired, read the New American translation of Psalms 34 and 54.

Chapters 9 and 10–In Which David Pleads His Case with King Saul

 Vocabulary
"Be thou *exalted*, O God . . ."   psaltery

 Comprehension Questions/Narration Prompts
1. How did God answer David's prayer for deliverance from King Saul in the wilderness of Maon?
2. How did David resolve the conflict between himself and King Saul?

 Forming Opinions/Drawing Conclusions
1. Give several reasons why David did not kill Saul when he had the opportunity. Would you have acted as David did? Explain your answer.
2. Imagine being hunted and pursued as David was by King Saul. What would the life of an outlaw have been like? Consider not only David but also his family and the men who traveled with him.

 For Further Study
David had great respect for King Saul, as he was a leader anointed by God. Read 1 Samuel (1 Kings) 8:1:22 on the establishment of the Israelite monarchy. Research this monarchy in a Catholic encyclopedia or online. How many kings reigned before the kingdom was divided? What caused this division and how long did it last? What were the functions of the kings? In your opinion, was the idea of an Israelite king a good idea? Explain. (See page 54 for more information on the kings of Israel.)

 Growing in Holiness
"It is not for us to judge anyone. . . . That task is the Lord's" (pages 55-56). Saul had brought chaos and misery to David's life, but David refused to judge Saul. Imitate David's nonjudgmental attitude by acknowledging that you cannot know someone else's true intentions. As difficult as it often is, do not judge others. Instead, imitate David.

 Geography
Add the following cities to your map: Maon and Engaddi (Engedi).

Searching Scripture
1. Read the continuing story of David and Saul in the Bible—1 Samuel (1 Kings) 23:25-24:23.
2. If desired, read the New American translation of Psalms 142 and 57. As you read these Psalms of David, keep in mind the context in which they were originally written and recited. Remember to pray the Psalms of David often, choosing psalms of thanksgiving and praise, or psalms of sorrow and petition depending on your current situation.

Chapters 11 and 12–In Which David Is Crowned King of Juda and Israel

 Vocabulary

give ear to my *supplication*
Forgive us for not paying you *homage*
pagan
idol(s)

 Comprehension Questions/Narration Prompts
1. After again being persecuted by King Saul, to whom did David turn?
2. What happened in Siceleg (Ziklag) when David and his men left?
3. What news caused a sword of sorrow to pierce David's heart?
4. How old was David when he was crowned king of Juda (Judah)? King of Israel?
5. How did God reward David for his childlike attitude in spiritual matters?

 Forming Opinions/Drawing Conclusions
1. If you had been with the men who returned to the ransacked Siceleg (Ziklag), would you have been one of those who criticized David? Would you have continued to support him as your leader? Why or why not?
2. What virtues or habits contributed to David's success as a great military commander?

 Growing in Holiness

We can learn three saintly lessons from King David in these chapters: first, be willing to admit your mistakes and apologize (page 66); secondly, live one day at a time and "do that day's work as well as possible" (page 70); and thirdly, never begin "any work without first asking His help" (page 70). Incorporate these lessons into your own spiritual life.

 Geography

Add to your map Siceleg (Ziklag), Hebron, and the provinces of Juda (Judah), Israel, Ammon, Edom, Negeb, and the land of the Philistines. Add too the Plain of Sharon.

 Timeline Work

Add the information from BC 1000 through BC 993 to your timeline.

📖 **Searching Scripture**
1. Research the Book of Psalms to determine the various authors. Note that approximately one-half of the psalms are attributed to David. Scan the 150 psalms, reading the title of each to determine which psalms were written by David.
2. If desired, read the New American translation of Psalms 143 and 101.
3. Read 1 Samuel (1 Kings) 29:1-30:19. Read too 2 Samuel (2 Kings) 1:1-2:4 and 5:1-5.

Chapters 13 and 14–In Which David Brings the Ark of the Covenant to Jerusalem and Commits a Great Sin

⟪REVIEW⟫ Vocabulary
the . . . *cavalcade* neared the gates
David received this *decree* calmly

Ark of the Covenant
hyssop

??? Comprehension Questions/Narration Prompts
1. After David captured the city of Jerusalem, what two things did he feel were lacking there?
2. What were the holiest possessions of the Israelites? How long before the reign of King David were these possessions obtained?
3. What did David discuss with his advisor Nathan? What did Nathan decide?
4. How was David tempted to commit a great sin? How did he react when confronted with his sin by Nathan?

Forming Opinions/Drawing Conclusions
1. Retell in your own words the story of the delivery of the Ark of the Covenant to Jerusalem.
2. ". . . because he has broken My Commandments . . ." (page 89). What commandments did David break regarding Urias (Uriah) and Bethsabee (Bathsheba)?

For Further Study
The Jews regard the kingdoms of David and Solomon as their history's golden age. Reseach this time period of religious history (1000 BC to 922 BC) and write a brief report. If you prefer, relate your findings in an oral presentation.

Growing in Holiness
"A small sin was a serious offense against so good a God" (page 89). Remember that not only are small sins serious offenses against God but, as illustrated by the devils' dialog in this chapter, they can be used to help us fall into bigger sins "without too much trouble" (page 86). Guard against even the smallest offense against our gracious God.

Geography
Add Jerusalem, Tyre, Samaria, and Sichem (Shechem) to your map.

Searching Scripture
1. Read about the Ark of the Covenant in 2 Samuel (2 Kings) 6:1-23, David's concern for the Ark in 2 Samuel (2 Kings) 7:1-17, and David's sin in 2 Samuel (2 Kings) 11:1-12:15.
2. If desired, read the New American translation of Psalms 24 and 51.

Chapters 15 and 16—In Which Absalom Forces David to Flee Jerusalem

 Vocabulary

helped the *prodigal* to his feet   *penitent*

 Comprehension Questions/Narration Prompts
1. What happened between King David's sons Amnon and Absalom?
2. Who caused David to flee the city of Jerusalem? What motivated him to go?
3. What kind of service did David ask of his trusted friend, Chusai (Hushai)?
4. What command did King David give to his army regarding his son Absalom?

 Forming Opinions/Drawing Conclusions
1. Summarize the "terrible news" of Chapter 15. What were some of the causes of this trouble? Is there anything David could have done to prevent this from happening?
2. ". . . [David] missed . . . the opportunity to spend a while in prayer before the Ark of the Covenant!" (page 107) If you could not spend time before Jesus in the Blessed tabernacle, would you miss him?

 Growing in Holiness

Are you as open to accepting God's "heaven-sent means for satisfying God's justice" (page 107) as David was? Imitate David by being quick to repent, and by willingly accepting trials and crosses as reparation for your sins and the sins of others.

 Geography

Add the region of Gessur (Geshur), the province of Galaad (Gilead), and the cities of Mahanaim, and Ephraim. Add the landmark sites of Gaza, Mt. Carmel, Nazareth, Cedes (Kedesh), Dan, Gomorrha (Gomorrah), and Sodom to complete the map.

✓ **Checking the Catechism**
"God . . . forgave [David's] sins. But David still had to be punished." (page 93) Older students may read the teachings of the *CCC* on temporal punishment in text paragraphs 1472-73 (310 and 312). Younger students may review temporal punishment, God's mercy, God's justice, penance, and reparation in their catechisms.

 Searching Scripture
1. ". . . helped the prodigal to his feet and embraced him warmly" (page 95) Read the story of the prodigal son in Luke 15:11-32.
2. Read 2 Samuel (2 Kings) 15:1-6, 13-18, and 30-37; 16:5-14; 17:15-16 and 22; and 18:1-5.
3. If desired, read the New American translation of Psalms 3 and 63.

Chapters 17 through 18–In Which David Prepares His Son Solomon for the Throne

---

 Vocabulary

fell into *scandalously* serious sin
fraught with many dangers

Jerusalem (Holy City)
sackcloth

 Comprehension Questions/Narration Prompts

1. What happened to Absalom after his forces lost the battle? How did David react? How did Joab justify his disobedience to King David's orders?
2. According to the census, how many soldiers were available to King David?
3. What three choices did God offer as punishment for David's pride? What did David choose? What was the cost of David's lesson in humility?
4. Which of David's son was to succeed him to the throne? What did David want his son to understand before he became king?

 Forming Opinions/Drawing Conclusions

1. "Again he fell into scandalously serious sin!" (page 114) Why was the taking of a census a serious sin of pride?
2. What events in David's life were lessons in humility for him? How can you apply these lessons to your own life?
3. Discuss the difference between pleasure and joy. (See page 121.)
4. List the lessons expressed in Psalm 37 (36) by paraphrasing each verse.

 Growing in Holiness

"How often during his own lifetime had he determined to root all his desires in God, and presently turned aside to seek his happiness in creatures, in possessions, in worldly amusements!" (page 121) The fleeting *pleasure* of worldly pursuits cannot compare to the lasting *joy* of eternal delights! Let us keep our eyes fixed on Jesus.

✓ **Checking the Catechism**

"... the king's conscience, more sensitive than that of most men ..." (page 116) Older students may read text paragraphs 1776-1802—especially 1776 and 1783-85—of the *CCC* (372-376). Younger students may review in their catechisms those sections that discuss the examination of conscience, and how to make a good confession. If desired, complete Activity #93, in *100 Activities Based on the Catechism of the Catholic Church*.

 Searching Scripture

1. Follow the story of David as related in the Bible by reading the following passages: 2 Samuel (2 Kings) 18:6-19:1 and 1 Chronicles (1 Paralipomenon) 21:1-22:19.
2. As quoted on page 115, read Exodus 30:11-16 regarding the census.
3. If desired, read the New American translation of Psalms 30 and 37.

Chapters 19 through 20–In Which Solomon Is Anointed King, and David Dies in Peace

 Vocabulary

Praise Him with *timbrel* and choir   *Messias* or *Messiah*

 Comprehension Questions/Narration Prompts
1. Which son of David's proclaimed himself king at Zoheleth? How did King David respond? How did the new king respond to his brother?
2. How did King David wish to spend his last strength?
3. What were the two kingdoms that Solomon pondered?

 Forming Opinions/Drawing Conclusions
"Poet, musician, soldier, statesman—David had been all of these" (page 134). What was David's greatest contribution to the world? Consider his capture of Jerusalem (still known as "the City of David"), his poems/psalms, his military victories, his founding of the kingdom of Israel, and his eternal covenant with God (as found in 2 Samuel [2 Kings] 7:8-16 and 23:5, Psalm 89 [88]:21-30, and Isaiah [Isaias] 55:3). Explain your answer.

 For Further Study
Research the temple in Jerusalem that was planned by David and built by Solomon. When was it completed? Name the various times it was destroyed and rebuilt. What is the approximate date of its final destruction?

 Growing in Holiness
". . . they were not merely giving *things* to God. They were giving *themselves*, their hearts and wills, in a great demonstration of love" (page 131). At the offertory of Mass, we give of our material *things* to God, but you can also offer *yourself* to God. "He cannot be outdone in generosity" (page 131). Remember that your will—your heart—is the greatest gift you can give Him.

 Timeline Work
Complete your timeline with events from the years BC 961 to BC 813.

 Searching Scripture
1. Read about Solomon's anointing in 1 (3) Kings 1:5-53. Also read the "Canticle of David" in 1 Chronicles (1 Paralipomenon) 29:10-13, then read to 29:30.
2. Read David's final advice to Solomon (paraphrased on pages 134-35) in 1 (3) Kings 2:1-5.
3. Read Psalm 150, the final doxology, and Solomon's Psalm 72 (71).
4. Solomon's building of the temple is described in 2 Chronicles (2 Paralipomenon) 1:18-4:22.

Kings and Prophets of the United and Divided Kingdoms

United Kingdom of Israel
Saul [1040-1000]   David [1000-961]   Solomon [961-922]

Kings of Israel
Jeroboam I [922-901]
Nadab [901-900]
Baasa (Baasha) [900-877]
Ela (Elah) [877-876]
Zambri (Zimri) [7 days - 876]
Amri (Omri) [876-869]
Achab (Ahab) [869-850]
  Elias (Elijah) [850]
Ochorias (Ahaziah) [850-849]
Joram (Jehoram) [849-843/2]
Jehu [843/2-815]
Joachaz (Joahaz) [815-801]
Joas (Joash/Jehoash) [802-786]
Jeroboam II [786-746]
  Amos [750]
  Osee (Hosea) [745]
Zacharias (Zechariah) [6 mos.- 746-745]
Sellum (Shallum) [1 mo. - 745]
Mahanem (Menahem) [745-737]
Phaceia (Pekahiah) [737-736]
Phacee (Pekah) [736-732]
Syro-Israelite Alliance [735-732]
Osee (Hoshea) [732-724]
Fall Of Samaria [722-721]

Kings of Judah
Roboam (Rehoboam) [922-915]
Abiam (Abijah/Abijam) [915-913]
Asa [913-873]
Josphat (Jehoshaphat) [873-849]
Joram (Jehoram) [849-843]
Ochozias (Ahaziah) [843/2]
Athalia (Athaliah) [842-837]
Joas (Joash) [837-800]
Amasias (Amaziah) [800-783]
Ozias/Azarius (Uzziah/Azariah) [783-742]
Joathan (Jotham) (regent) [750-742]
Jothan (Jotham) (king) [742-735]
  Isaias (Isaiah) [742-700]
Achaz (Jehoahaz/Ahaz) [735-715]
Invasion By Syro-Israelite Alliance [735]
  Micheas (Micah) [before 722-701]
Ezechias (Hezekiah) [715-687/6]
Manasses (Manasseh) [687/6-642]
Amon [642-640]
Josias (Josiah) [640-609]
  Sophonias (Zephaniah) [628-622]
  Jeermias (Jeremiah) [626-587]
Joachaz/Jechonias (Jehoahaz II/Shallum) [3 mos.- 609]
Joakim/Eliakim (Jehoiakim/Eliakim) [609-598/7]
  Habacuc (Habakkuk) [605]
Joachinor/Jechonias (Jehoiachin/Jeconiah) [3 mos.- 598-597]
First Deportation To Babylonia
Sedecias (Zedekiah/Mattaniah) [597-587]
Fall Of Jerusalem, Second Deportation [587]
Babylonian Exile [587-538]
  Ezechiel (Ezekiel) [593-573]
  Second Isaias (Isaiah) [540]
  Aggeus and Zacharias (Haggai and Zechariah) [520-515]
  Malachias (Malachi) [500-450]

(Note: All dates are BC. Prophets are in Italics. Where names are different, Douay-Rheims names are first with New American names in parenthesis. Expect some date and name variations from source to source. Dates are taken from Bernhard W. Anderson's *Understanding the Old Testament*, © 1998.)

Book Summary Test for *King David and His Songs*

Directions: Answer in complete sentences. If necessary, use the back page for additional writing space. (100 possible points, 20 points for each answer)

1. What did the prophet Samuel do when he met David? What was David's job with his father? How did he pass the time in this job?

   _____
   _____
   _____

2. What did David do that made him a hero in the eyes of his countrymen? How did King Saul react to this?

   _____
   _____

3. Name at least two great accomplishments of King David.

   _____
   _____

4. Who succeeded King David as King of Israel and Juda (Judah)? What project of King David's did he complete?

   _____
   _____

5. What saintly lessons did you learn from this story of King David? How will you incorporate these lessons into your own spiritual life?

   _____
   _____
   _____
   _____

King David and His Songs, A Story of the Psalms
Answer Key to Comprehension Questions

Chapters 1 through 3 – In Which Samuel Anoints David
1. Isai (Jesse) of Bethlehem had eight sons; David was the youngest and a boy of fifteen when Samuel came to him.
2. When Samuel met David, he offered a brief prayer and anointed David's head with holy oil.
3. David's favorite pastime was playing the flute. David "knew many songs, some handed down from one generation to another, others which he had composed himself" (page 3). (Note that the period from Moses to David was a period of oral tradition. The songs that David knew had been handed down not as written records but as oral tradition. Some written records do exist before the time of David, and some traditions after David were handed down orally; but it was about the time of David that written records became more common. Ancient people practiced the art of "learning by heart" those poems, proverbs, and stories that were meaningful to them. We tend to rely almost exclusively upon the written word. See Timeline on page 42 for more information regarding the introduction of the alphabet.)
4. David went to Saul upon the request of King Saul himself. Saul was having trouble eating and sleeping and hoped that David's music would soothe and relax him. David played for Saul on the harp and sang for him. Saul grew fond of David and made him his armor-bearer.

Chapters 4 through 6—In Which David Kills Goliath, and Saul Grows Envious of David
1. David gave all the credit for his victory over Goliath to God, ". . . today's victory belongs to God. . . . Without His help, I could have done nothing" (page 21).
2. Immediately after David's victory over Goliath, Saul threw a great banquet for David. He was very grateful to David and treated him, as did everyone else, as a true hero. However as time went on, Saul grew envious of David's popularity with the Hebrew people. Saul's jealousy and rage grew to the point that he was planning to harm David.
3. Saul's hatred of David grew to such an extent that several times he lost his temper and threw a spear at David with the intention of hurting or even killing David. Jonathan tried to talk to his father, King Saul, in order to convince him that David loved Saul and did not intend to take the throne away from him.

Chapters 7 and 8—In Which David Escapes King Saul and Lives as a Fugitive
1. David escaped from King Saul by climbing out through a window at night and evading the king's guarding soldiers.
2. David felt uneasy after he left Nobe's (Nob's) high priest, Achimelech (Ahimelech), as he had told the high priest several lies. In addition, King Saul's chief herdsman, Doeg, had seen him in Nobe.
3. After allowing himself to be captured by the Philistines, David lost courage and realized that he had made a mistake in going to the Philistines. He escaped by glaring wildly and rolling on the ground in a pretend fit of madness.
4. After escaping the Philistines, David moved from place to place to avoid capture by King Saul. He lived in a large cave near Bethlehem, in Moab, in the forest of Haret (Hereth), fought the Philistines in Ceila (Keilah), and then moved to the desert of Ziph.

Chapters 9 and 10—In Which David Pleads His Case with King Saul
1. In the wilderness of Maon, when David seemed trapped by King Saul and his army, God answered David's prayer for deliverance by bringing news to King Saul that the Philistines had attacked Israel. King Saul immediately left in order to do battle with the Philistines.
2. David resolved the conflict between himself and King Saul not by killing King Saul (although he had the opportunity to do so) but by contritely reminding Saul how devoted he had been to him. David informed King Saul that in his mercy he had spared King Saul's life.

Chapters 11 and 12—In Which David Is Crowned King of Juda and Israel
1. After again being persecuted by King Saul, David turned to the Philistines in his attempt to secure peace.
2. When David and his men left Siceleg (Ziklag), the Amalecite (Amalekite) tribe descended upon the city, capturing the women and children as well as all of the flocks. They then set fire to the houses and public buildings.
3. A sword of sorrow pierced David's heart when he was told that Jonathan was among those killed in the battle between the Israelites and the Philistines.
4. David was thirty years old when he was crowned king of Juda (Judah) and thirty-seven years old when he became king of Israel as well.
5. God rewarded David for his childlike attitude in spiritual matters by granting David the extraordinary favor of uttering prayers, or songs, that God himself composed—prayers that have been prayed ever since from the Book of Psalms.

Chapters 13 and 14—In Which David Brings the Ark of the Covenant to Jerusalem and Commits a Great Sin
1. King David captured the city of Jerusalem, but he felt that two things were lacking there—the Ark of the Covenant and a "magnificent temple in which to shelter it" (page 76).
2. The holiest possessions of the Israelites were the stone tablets containing the Ten Commandments given to Moses four hundred years before the reign of King David.
3. King David discussed with his advisor Nathan the possibility of building a temple in Jerusalem befitting the Ark of the Covenant. However, Nathan prayerfully decided that it was not David who should undertake the building of this temple, but rather his son who would succeed him as king.
4. David, as a poet and musician, was attracted to beauty and goodness. He was tempted to desire a beautiful woman who was already married. He sinned in this desire as well as in his method of obtaining that desire. When confronted by Nathan with his sin, David was grievously sorrowful.

Chapters 15 and 16—In Which Absalom Forces David to Flee Jerusalem
1. After a quarrel, King David's son Absalom murdered his brother Amnon. Absalom fled for refuge to Gessur.
2. Absalom caused David to flee Jerusalem by proclaiming himself King of Israel and marching in revolution with his soldiers on Jerusalem. David was willing to let his son wear the crown without bloodshed rather than allow Absalom to commit the "terrible sin of killing his own father" (page 99), or to have the city laid to waste and have innocent men killed in battle.
3. David asked his trusted friend, Chusai (Hushai), to return to Jerusalem to win Absalom's confidence and to outwit Absalom's chief advisor, Achitophel (Ahithophel).
4. As David's and Absalom's forces prepared for battle, King David ordered that his son Absalom not be harmed in battle but be brought to King David alive and unharmed.

Chapters 17 and 18—In Which David Prepares His Son Solomon for the Throne
1. After the loss of over 20,000 men, Absalom's forces retreated in defeat against the troops of King David. Joab, David's nephew, killed Absalom. He justified his disobedience to the king's command not to harm Absalom by stating that the kingdom would never know peace as long as Absalom was alive. David was deeply grieved over Absalom's death, which David believed to be further punishment for his own sins.
2. According to the census, 800,000 soldiers were available to King David in the provinces of Israel and 500.000 more in the provinces of Juda (Judah) for a total of 1.3 million soldiers.
3. God offered three choices of punishment for David's prideful sin in conducting the census: a seven-year famine, three months' flight from his enemies, or three days of destroying pestilence. David chose pestilence which resulted in the death of 70,000 people—a severe price for David's lesson in humility.
4. David's son Solomon, son of Bethsabee (Bathsheba), was to succeed him to the throne. In preparation for his reign as king, David wanted Solomon to "learn to put his whole trust in

King David and His Songs

God and seek his happiness only in Him" (page 121). David also wanted Solomon to learn two important truths: "that it is only the just man who can know real peace"; and "that the unjust, no matter what his apparent good fortune, is doomed to misery and failure!" (page 121).

Chapters 19 and 20—In Which Solomon Is Anointed King, and David Dies in Peace

1. David's fourth son, Adonias (Adonijah) who was next in line after Absalom, proclaimed himself king at Zoheleth. He had the support of the high priest Abiathar and David's nephew Joab. King David responded immediately by having Solomon—"whom God had chosen to be king" (page 127)—anointed as king followed by a great procession and feast. King Solomon acted mercifully toward to his brother, preventing a civil war such as had occurred between David and Absalom.
2. King David wished to spend his last strength "in the service of God" (page 129). He made a great speech requesting loyalty to Solomon, praising God, accusing himself of his sins, and requesting support for the great temple to be built.
3. After the death of King David, Solomon pondered not only his own Kingdom of Israel but also the promised Kingdom of the Messias (Messiah).

Answer Key to Test

1. When the prophet Samuel met David, he prayed over him. He anointed David's head with holy oil, making him the secret successor of King Saul. David had been called in from the field where he had been tending his father's sheep, which was David's daily responsibility. While tending the sheep, David often passed the time by singing songs to God and playing the flute (as well as other musical instruments).
2. David became a hero in the eyes of his countrymen when he killed the Philistine Goliath and prevented a war between the Philistines and Israel. At first, King Saul rejoiced at this victory. Later, he grew jealous of David's popularity and began to see David as a threat to his power and to his throne.
3. David had several great accomplishments as King of Israel and Juda (Judah). He was a poet, a musician, a political leader, and a great military commander. He captured the city of Jerusalem from the Philistines and established it as the religious capital of all Israel. (Jerusalem is often called the "City of David.") He was a capable ruler of Israel and was faithful to God. He wrote many songs, which have been recorded in the Book of Psalms. He collected materials for the great temple of Jerusalem that his successor was to build.
4. King David's son Solomon, son of David's wife Bethsabee (Bathsheba), became the third King of Israel after the death of David. King Solomon completed the great temple of Jerusalem that was envisioned by his father David [1 Kings (3 Kings) 6:1-38]. [He also extended Israel's borders, built a magnificent royal palace—1 Kings (3 Kings) 7:1, extended trade, and wrote many songs and proverbs—1 Kings (3 Kings) 5:12. King Solomon wrote much of the Book of Proverbs. Jewish people regard the kingdom of David and Solomon as their golden age. After King Solomon's reign, the kingdom was divided. See page 54 of this guide for more information on the kings and prophets of the United and Divided Kingdoms.]
5. Answers will vary.

Note on Personal and Geographical Names in the Bible

In comparing the text of the Douay-Rheims (DR) and New American (NA) translations of the Bible, readers will note that many of the names of people as well as places vary in spelling. For example, *Juda* in the DR translation is *Judah* in the NA Bible, and *Bethsabee* is *Bathsheba*. Some of these variations (such as *Juda* and *Judah*) are simply spelling variations. Other variances, such as *Jesse* (NA) and *Isai* (DR), derive from the translation of the Hebrew word (*Isai*) into its Greek counterpart (*Jesse*). Thus, the Grecized *Judah* or *Juda* is *Judea*. Remember that the Douay-Rheims translation comes from the Latin Vulgate whereas the New American translation comes directly from the Hebrew, Aramaic or Greek text (as the case may be for the specific book). Within this study guide, the personal and geographical names of the Douay-Rheims translation are used—as in the text of the Windeatt biography. When these names differ from those of the New American translation, the New American version appears in parentheses.

Study Guide for

*Blessed Marie of
New France, The Story
of the First Missionary
Sisters in Canada*

Blessed Marie of New France

Marie Guyart Martin, from the age of fourteen,
A nun's life desired, of this she was keen.
Her parents weren't sure
If she was mature.
Her dad had her married—she was seventeen.

Her husband died soon after birth of son Claude.
Though penniless and grieving, her shoulders were broad.
By herself raised her son,
The respect of all won.
But still she was restless and wished to serve God.

To the Ursuline convent against every odd,
Her son missed her awfully, her sister did prod.
A nun she stayed still,
Felt it was God's will.
Through dreams she determined foreign lands she would trod.

Through trial and adversity, with patience the key,
At last she set sail for New France 'cross the sea.
When there kissed the ground,
A convent to found,
To teach and save souls were the goals of Marie.

Conditions of wilderness—privations and cold
Marie learned the language, students enrolled.
War always a threat;
She had no regret.
Her son joined the priesthood, of this she was told.

She taught children of natives, French children to pray.
Learned contemplation, true grit did display.
Her legacy lives on
As fresh as the dawn.
Still in Montreal are the Ursulines today.

Think what you can learn from this saint and her tale.
How you can apply it to help you prevail.
Then mold what you do
And boldly pursue
Her pattern of holiness. Follow her trail.

NOTE: Blessed Marie was canonized by Pope Francis on April 3, 2014. For purposes of consistency with the biography, references to St. Marie will remain as "Blessed" in this study guide.

Timeline of Events

Year	Event
1535-1536	Jacques Cartier sails to New France (Canada) and explores the St. Lawrence River, claiming Canada for France
1582	Death of St. Teresa of Avila; water wheels installed on London Bridge
1596	Ursuline order is established in France by St. Francois de Bermond (1572-1628); Galileo invents the thermometer
1599	On October 28, birth of Marie Guyart (Blessed Marie Guyard of the Incarnation—see Historical Note in *Blessed Marie of New France*.)
1608	First successful Canadian settlement established at Quebec by Samuel de Champlain
1610	Discovery of Lake Champlain; death of King Henry IV of Navarre, France
1614	Pocahontas marries John Rolfe
1617	Marie Guyart marries Claude Martin; Pocahontas dies
1619	On April 2, birth of son Claude Martin; death of Marie Martin's husband, Claude, in October; William Harvey discovers the circulation of blood
1620	Birth of St. Marguerite Bourgeoys; *Mayflower* lands at New Plymouth, MA
1631	Marie enters the Ursuline convent in Tour, France, on January 25
1634	Catholic colony established in the United States in Maryland
1636	Marie appointed Assistant Novice Mistress; founding of Harvard University
1639	Marie leaves Dieppe, France, for Canada on May 4, arriving in Quebec, on August 1
1640	Foundation for three-story house laid (It took almost three years to complete.)
1641	Claude joins the Benedictine Congregation of St. Maur on January 15 (ordained a priest on November 10, 1649)
1642	Death of Dr. Renè Goupil; death of Galileo Galilei; priests outlawed in VA
1646	Death of St. Isaac Jogues; Rembrandt paints "Adoration of the Shepherds"
1648	Peace of Westphalia ends the Thirty Years' War in Europe
1650	December 30, convent house burns—total loss; new house started on May 19, 1651, and completed in the spring of 1653
1652	Death of Mère St. Joseph on April 4; minuet dance comes into fashion
1658	John Milton begins writing his epic poem *Paradise Lost*
1659	Arrival of Francois de Montmorency-Laval as Bishop of Quebec on June 16
1660	Battle of the Long Sault between Adam Dollard (and his companions) and the Iroquois in April; St. Louise de Marillac dies
1665	First modern census taken in Quebec; bubonic plague strikes London
1666	Peace established between the French colonists and the Iroquois nation; first cheddar cheese made; Antonio Stradivari starts to make violins
1668	Isaac Newton invents the reflecting telescope
1670	Death of St. Marguerite Bourgeoys, foundress of the Sisters of the Congregation of Notre Dame in Montreal; incorporation of Hudson Bay Company
1671	Death of Madame de la Peltrie on November 18 of hepatitis
1672	On April 30, death of Mère Marie—who was declared venerable in April 1922, and beautified by Pope John Paul II on June 22, 1980
1682	William Penn founds Quaker colony in PA; LaSalle explores Louisiana
1683	First Catholic chapel established in New York City
1696	Death of Mère Marie's son Claude Martin; Russia conquers Kamchatka
2014	Canonization of Marie Guyart of the Incarnation ("Mother of the Canadian Church") by Pope Francis on April 3. Francois de Montmorency-Laval (second bishop of North America) was also canonized on this day.

Chapter 1–In Which Madame Marie Martin Joins the Ursulines

 Vocabulary

pale-faced and *woebegone*
resolutely crossed the *threshold*

Monseigneur (Monsignor)
Ursulines

 Comprehension Questions/Narration Prompts
1. Why did the archbishop summon Madame Martin to see him?
2. Describe the dream that Madame Martin had as a child.
3. How old was Madame Martin when she entered the Ursuline convent?

 Forming Opinions/Drawing Conclusions
1. Describe Madame Martin's business experience. Why was her brother-in-law opposed to her entrance into the Ursuline convent?
2. Madame Buisson speaks of the dozens of workers that Madame Martin has helped "return to the Sacraments" (page 11). What does this phrase mean?

 For Further Study
This biography begins in the year of 1631 in France before Blessed Marie travels to New France. However, two French explorers had already explored the northern region of North America. Research the lives and Canadian explorations of Jacques Cartier (1491-1557) and Samuel de Champlain (1567-1635). As time allows, research the lives of Father Pierre Marquette and the Italian explorer, John Cabot.

 Growing in Holiness
We all can name people who claim to be Catholic but do not attend Mass regularly or actively practice their faith. Imitate Blessed Marie by speaking to someone you know to encourage their "return to the sacraments." Additionally, pray, fast, and sacrifice for them. Pray for the conversion of a great many sinners!

 Geography
Trace the map of France found on page 63 of this study guide. Color these seas, oceans, and rivers blue: Atlantic, North, Mediterranean, Bay of Biscay, Rhine, and Danube. Color the Pyrenees Mountains brown. (The map will be completed in Chapter 4.)

Searching Scripture
Find the following phrases in the book of Luke: "Hail . . . the Lord is with you," and "Blessed are you among women" (page 16).

Chapter 2–In Which Mére Marie Dreams of Becoming a Missionary

 Vocabulary

in a *niche* above the entrance
crippled with *rheumatism*
refectory
Jesuits

 Comprehension Questions/Narration Prompts
1. What distracted Sister Marie in her early days as an Ursuline?
2. What were the trials that Sister Marie discussed with the Novice Mistress?
3. What schools did Claude attend? How successful was he at each one?
4. Why did the Jesuits request that teaching nuns be sent to New France?

 Forming Opinions/Drawing Conclusions
1. Retell the dream about New France that Mère Marie had in early 1635.
2. Name some difficulties Mère Marie had to overcome as a missionary in New France.

 For Further Study

The Jesuit *Relations* is a detailed account of the Jesuit missionary activity from 1610-1791. All 71 volumes have been translated into English and can be read online at http://puffin.creighton.edu/jesuit/relations. Blessed Marie's readings of the 1635 accounts are contained in Volumes 7 and 8. Marie's contributions to the *Relations* can be viewed by searching for "Incarnation," especially in Volumes 19 and 38.

 Growing in Holiness

Cartier named the St. Lawrence River after St. Lawrence whose feast was on the day of its discovery. Obtain a Catholic calendar, and develop the habit of asking the assistance of the saint of the day even if it is only calling upon his/her name and saying each morning, "St. _____, pray for us."

Timeline Work

Taping sheets of plain paper end-to-end, make a timeline representing the years from 1535 through 1696. Let three inches equal 25 years. Mark on your timeline the dates and events from 1535 through 1634, using information from page 62 of this study guide.

✓ **Checking the Catechism**

". . . win for us the very virtues we think we'll never have!" (page 20) Older students may read text paragraphs 1803-1813 (159, 263, 377-388, and 558) of the *Catechism of the Catholic Church (CCC)*. Younger students may review the following terms: virtue, cardinal or moral virtues, and theological or supernatural virtues.

Chapter 3–In Which Mère Marie Waits for Her Dream to Come True

 Vocabulary

play on the *viol*
asked Jean de Bernières *jovially*
rector
Veni Creator

 Comprehension Questions/Narration Prompts
1. Who was Madame Marie Madeleine de la Peltrie?
2. What were some of the hardships endured by missionaries to Canada?
3. After waiting for four years, Mère Marie was on her way to New France. How much notice did she have when the time came to leave?

 Forming Opinions/Drawing Conclusions
1. Pierre stated that Monsieur Bernières had the "face of a saint" (page 39). What might this face look like? What does it mean to have the ability to "read my soul"? (page 39)
2. What aspects of her life up until this point had helped prepare Mère Marie for the lifestyle she experienced in New France?
3. What do you think Monsieur Bernières' "trouble in Orlèans" might be?

 For Further Study

Research the history of *Veni Creator Spiritus* ("Come, Creator Spirit"). To whom is this hymn attributed? When was it written? On what occasions is this hymn often sung?

 Growing in Holiness

Madame de la Peltrie tells Mère Marie of her promise to St. Joseph (page 42). Remember that any power the saints have come from their intimate union with Christ. As God's special friends, they are powerful intercessors that we can call on to aid us in our journey toward heaven. Cultivate a special relationship with the Blessed Mother as well as your own patron saint.

✓ **Checking the Catechism**

Older students may read text paragraphs 437, 497, 532, 1014, 1846, and 2177 (104) in the *CCC* regarding St. Joseph. Younger students should also review any lessons relative to St. Joseph in their catechisms.

 Searching Scripture

Chapter 3 shows Mère Marie waiting for God to provide the opportunity to go to New France. Read about waiting in the following biblical passages: Genesis 29: 13-20, Psalm 33 (32):20-22, Isaiah 64:4b (Isaias 64:3b), James 5:7-8, and Jude 20-21.

Chapter 4–In Which Mère Marie Tells Claude of Her Missionary Plans

Vocabulary

got nowhere with such *tactics* *archbishop*
hasn't the slightest *notion* *martyrdom*

Comprehension Questions/Narration Prompts
1. What tactics did Mère Marie's sister, Madame Buisson, employ in her attempt to keep Mère Marie from going to New France?
2. Who was waiting for Mère Marie when she arrived at the inn in Orlèans?
3. What news regarding Claude Martin did Mère Marie and her companions receive upon their arrival in Paris?

Forming Opinions/Drawing Conclusions
1. With the advantage of hindsight, brainstorm for ideas on what Mère Marie might have done differently to break the news of her assignment in New France to her son Claude. (Remember that email or telephone would not have been an option!)
2. In your opinion, why might the Jesuits at Paris not accept Claude as a candidate for the priesthood?

Growing in Holiness
Several times within the last two chapters, Ms. Windeatt has put the phrase, "God be praised!" into the thoughts of Mère Marie (pages 41 and 55). Incorporate this holy habit into your own life. For each blessing received—both small and large—take time to praise and thank God. Use this short prayer often.

Geography
Complete the map of France started in Chapter 1 by labeling all cities red and the four countries green. On the map provided, cities are indicated with a star, and countries are in bold capitals.

For Further Study
Research the religious order of the Society of Jesus—the Jesuits—to whom Claude applied for admission to the priesthood. Who was the founder of this order? When was it founded? What was its original two-fold purpose?

Searching Scripture
Read about God's holy will in the following passages from Sacred Scripture: Wisdom 9:9, Romans 12:2, Ephesians 5: 6-17, and Hebrews 10:36.

Chapter 5–In Which Mére Marie Arrives in New France

 Vocabulary

beyond the *prow* of the ship
in *league* with the English

Little Office of the Blessed Virgin
general absolution

 Comprehension Questions/Narration Prompts
1. Upon what did the missionaries feel that their success in Canada depended?
2. What reason did Monsieur Bernières give for staying in France?
3. With what did the *Saint Joseph* nearly collide on the way to New France?

 Forming Opinions/Drawing Conclusions
1. In what ways might the ship's crew and passengers fulfill their vow to serve our Lady "for the rest of their days"? (page 68)
2. What do you think of Captain Bontemps' opinion of the tribes of Canada?

 For Further Study
1. Research the various Native American tribes mentioned in this chapter: Algonquin, Iroquois, Mohawks, Oneidas, Onondagas, Cayugas, and Senecas. Where did each tribe live? What was their lifestyle? For what was each tribe known?
2. Charlotte and Madame de la Peltrie speak of the birth of the future King Louis XIV. Research the life and rule of this king. How old was he when he assumed the crown? Why was he known as the "Sun King"?

 Growing in Holiness
Mère Marie felt that "from all eternity He had planned that she should tell the little ones of Canada about Himself" (page 70). God also has had plans for you from all eternity. Assess your strengths and weaknesses, and try to discern how you might best serve Him. Remember to pray daily that you may fulfill His unique plan for you.

 Geography
Using a modern map of Canada, locate the following water landmarks: Atlantic Ocean, Labrador Sea, Davis Strait, Hudson Strait, St. Lawrence River, Hudson Bay, Gulf of St. Lawrence, and each of the five Great Lakes.

Searching Scripture
Read Isaiah's proclamation of God's care for those who travel the sea in Isaiah (Isaias) 43:16. Read too about Jonah's (Jonas') journey by ship in Jonah (Jonas) Chapter 1. Paul's perilous journey by sea is narrated in Acts 27:1-44.

Chapter 6–In Which Mère Marie and Her Companions Arrive in Quebec

 Vocabulary

conditions . . . were *deplorable*
began his *address* of welcome

Augustinians
procession

 Comprehension Questions/Narration Prompts
1. What was the "great consolation" that Mère Marie and her companions had while onboard the *Saint Jacques*?
2. What was the population of Quebec in 1639 when Mère Marie arrived?
3. What type of reception did the nuns receive upon their arrival in Quebec?

 Forming Opinions/Drawing Conclusions
1. Placing yourself in Mère Marie's situation, describe the feelings you might have had on your first night in Quebec.
2. The Jesuit priests went to Canada to preach and offer the sacraments. The Augustinian nuns went to open a hospital. The Ursuline nuns went to teach the children. Each religious order has a different role in fulfilling God's plan. Which of these three roles do you think is the most important? To which order would you like to belong? Which of these three ways of evangelization do you feel the most called to do?

For Further Study
Mère St. Joseph, always the comical one, nicknamed their two-room cottage "The Louvre," after "the famous palace in France" (page 81). For what is the palace now famous? When was it built and by whom? Where is it located?

 Growing in Holiness
Mère Marie and her companions did not complain about the fish stored in their quarters on the boat. When you are tempted to complain, remember Blessed Marie's example. Always try to look on the bright side of any situation. Smile instead of grumble!

✓ **Checking the Catechism**
Older students may read about religious families and the consecrated life in text paragraphs 917-933 (192-193) of the *CCC*. If desired, complete Activity #79 in *100 Activities Based on the Catechism of the Catholic Church*. Younger students may research various religious orders, and review the Sacrament of Holy Orders and the idea of "vocation."

📖 **Searching Scripture**
Mère Marie planned to build the convent "two hundred feet up the sheer cliff" (page 82). Read about a house built on rock in Matthew 7:24-27.

Chapter 7—In Which Mère Marie Makes a Great Sacrifice

Vocabulary
when *smallpox* broke out
His companion ... nodded *ruefully*
apostle
Benedictines

 Comprehension Questions/Narration Prompts
1. What reasons did Père Le Jeune give Mère Marie regarding the importance of teaching the children their Christian faith?
2. What disease swept through New France during the winter of 1639-40?
3. What sacrifice did God require of Mère Marie in the spring of 1642? For whom did she offer this sacrifice?

 Forming Opinions/Drawing Conclusions
1. "Who cared about bear grease or fleas, when the newly baptized Marie had a soul that was as pure as snow?" (pages 84-85) Name several times that you have failed to see the true value of someone due to his or her outward appearance. On a practical level, what does it mean to see the face of Christ in everyone?
2. Explain how Mère Marie felt when Madame de la Peltrie decided to leave for Montreal? How might you have felt?

 For Further Study
1. Mère Marie and her companions learned to speak and write in both the Huron and Algonquin languages. Learn several prayers—including the Our Father, Hail Mary and Sign of the Cross—in Latin. If you are familiar with another language such as Spanish or French, learn these prayers in that language as well.
2. Read Agnes Repplier's biography, *Mère Marie of the Ursulines*, which provides information regarding other historical characters and events in New France. This 1951 book is readily available from used bookstores.

 Growing in Holiness
Mère Marie's commitment to her son's priestly vocation was so strong that she was willing to cheerfully undergo great sacrifices for him. Resolve to regularly offer up some suffering of your own as a sacrifice for an increase in good and holy Catholic priests in your diocese. Adapt the prayer of Mère Marie's on page 96 for this purpose.

Geography
Locate the following landmarks on a map of Canada: Nova Scotia, the city of Quebec, the city of Montreal, the city of Trois Rivières, Greenland, Newfoundland, the Baffin Islands, and the capital city of Ottawa.

Chapter 8–In Which the Ursulines Move into Their New Convent

 Vocabulary

had left their *haunts*
good red *serge* in the storeroom

Sacred Heart of Jesus
Divine Providence

 Comprehension Questions/Narration Prompts
1. Why was Mère Marie worried about Madame de la Peltrie in Montreal?
2. When did the Ursulines move into their new convent?
3. What events occurred that brought Madame de la Peltrie back to Quebec?

 Forming Opinions/Drawing Conclusions
1. Why did Père Lalemant believe that Madame de la Peltrie did not have a religious vocation? What characteristics may be indicators of a religious vocation?
2. ". . . God's plans always work out perfectly, especially if we don't struggle against them" (page 112). What are some ways that we can—and do—struggle against God's plans? What can you do to help prevent this?

 For Further Study
"Certainly Mère Marie's the first person I ever knew who thought of paying honor to Jesus in His Sacred Heart" (page 103). This feast was first celebrated in Mère Marie's monastery on June 18, 1700, only twelve years after the final revelation to St. Margaret Mary Alacoque in France. Research the history of devotion to the Sacred Heart of Jesus.

 Growing in Holiness
What does it mean to be "poorer than Our Lady was on the first Christmas night"? (page 99) How does this expression help us to keep our material wealth in perspective? Share some of your possessions today with someone less fortunate.

 Timeline Work
Add the dates and events from 1636 through 1650 to your timeline.

✓ **Checking the Catechism**
Madame de la Peltrie felt the call to be a missionary. Related text paragraphs in the *CCC* may be read by older students: 1122, 1533, and 2044 (80, 172, and 190). Younger students may read a short biography of any missionary saint of their choice.

 Searching Scripture
Read what Holy Scripture teaches us about the mission to all nations: Matthew 28:19-20, Luke 24:46-47, and Acts 1:8.

Chapter 9–In Which the Ursulines of Quebec Suffer Two Great Losses

 Vocabulary

myriad of glittering stars
these *delicacies* would tempt her

ordained
monastery

 Comprehension Questions/Narration Prompts
1. When did the fire occur in Mère Marie's convent in Quebec?
2. Where did the Ursulines take up temporary quarters after the fire?
3. What happened on April 4, 1652?

 Forming Opinions/Drawing Conclusions
1. Why were fires so common—and so devastating—in the 17th century?
2. "The sufferings it brought are only part of God's plan. I know they'll win many blessings" (page 118). Do you believe that sufferings can bring blessings? Explain. How can we use this knowledge to decrease our whiney and complaining spirits?

 For Further Study
1. Research the lives of Fr. Isaac Jogues, Renè Goupil, Charles Garnier, Noël Chabanel, Jean de la Lande, Antoine Daniel, and Jean de Brébeuf—all contemporaries of Blessed Marie of the Incarnation. Although there seemed to be very little fruit from these martyers' labors, in 1656 (now St.) Kateri Tekawitha was born into a small, struggling Christian community in the very village where St. Isaac Jogues was martyred.
2. Research the Ursuline monastery in Quebec. Note the destruction caused by another fire in 1686. When was the last structure built? Is the convent still active?

 Growing in Holiness
"Don't let us question His holy will in any way" (pages 118 and 123). Examine your own life. In what ways have you questioned or ignored God's will for you? When have you accepted His will? What can you do to become more open to God's will for your life?

✓ **Checking the Catechism**
Mère St. Joseph asked her Ursuline community, "You will pray for me when I'm gone?" (page 120). Older students may read text paragraphs 1030-32 and 1472 (210-211 and 312) on the doctrine of Purgatory in the *CCC*. Younger students may review Purgatory, indulgences, and the spiritual works of mercy in their catechisms.

 Searching Scripture
Read biblical passages relating to Purgatory and prayers for the dead: 2 Maccabees (2 Machabees) 12:38-46, 1 Corinthians 3:15, and Revelation (Apocalypse) 21:27 and 22:14-15.

Chapter 10–In Which the Iroquois Trouble the French Colonists

 Vocabulary
could not *surmount* a difficulty *Sulpician*
The *garrisons* at Montreal and Quebec *Te Deum*

 Comprehension Questions/Narration Prompts
1. How did Mère Marie manage to remain in the monastery during the time of danger?
2. Why did the bishop feel that the unrest between the Iroquois and the French colonists was the fault of the current French king, King Louis XIV?
3. What was the result of the peace established between the French colonists and the Iroquois nation?

 Forming Opinions/Drawing Conclusions
1. Bishop de Montmorency-Laval calls Mère Marie a "delightful diplomat" (page 126). Why does he use this term? What are the characteristics of an effective diplomat?
2. Why was the Blessed Sacrament from the Ursuline monastery removed to the Jesuit stronghold?
3. Describe the battle between Adam Dollard' forces and the Iroquois at Sault Saint Louis in April 1660. (This battle can be compared to the United States' Battle of the Alamo.)

 For Further Study
Research the lives of two important Catholics in the history of Canada that are mentioned in this chapter: Bishop Francois de Montmorency-Laval (Bishop of Quebec from 1674 to 1688) and Marguerite Bourgeoys (1620-1670).

 Growing in Holiness
Throughout this chapter, the French colonists pray for their troops. Adopt this holy habit by praying frequently for American troops stationed throughout the world. Remember too those troops who have died protecting your freedom.

✓ **Checking the Catechism**
Mère Marie calls upon our "Father in Heaven" to give the French troops strength (page 135). Older students may read about God the Father in the *CCC* in text paragraphs 232-242 (46, 48, 52, 122, 130, 132, 154, 221, and 582-584). Complete Activities #75 and #76 in *100 Activities*. Younger students may review the Trinity and creation in their catechisms.

 Searching Scripture
Read the following passages on the importance of relying on the Lord in battle: Deuteronomy 20:1-4, Joshua (Josue) 23:10, Psalm 27 (26):1-3, and Romans 10:13.

Chapter 11—In Which Mère Marie Is Taken to Her Heavenly Reward

 Vocabulary

finally *rousing* herself
turned him down *pointblank*

excommunicate
odor of sanctity (from Historical Note)

 Comprehension Questions/Narration Prompts
1. With what trade practice of the French colonists did Mère Marie disagree?
2. In 1670, what did Mère Marie request regarding her role in the Ursuline community? What were her duties in the later years of her life?
3. To what did Monsieur Talon attribute Claude Martin's success as a scholar and priest?

 Forming Opinions/Drawing Conclusions
1. Why was the baptism of Iroquois Chief Barakontié such a monumental event?
2. Explain Mère Marie's analogy of the grave as a place for old clothes.

 For Further Study
Research the Shrine of St. Anne in Beaupré, Quebec. By what other name is the Statue of St. Anne known? What are the four relics preserved at the shrine? When was the privilege of "basilica" bestowed upon the shrine?

 Growing in Holiness
Throughout her life, Mère Marie wrote many letters describing life in New France as well as revealing her own spiritual life. Write a letter to someone you know to share something spiritual with him/her. Or begin to keep a spiritual journal, writing in it daily of your experiences, resolutions, and insights.

 Timeline Work
Add events from 1652 through 1696 to complete your timeline.

✓ **Checking the Catechism**
Older students may read what the *CCC* teaches about the resurrection of the body in text paragraphs 364 and 988-991 (131, 202-205, and 214). If desired, complete Activity #33 in *100 Activities*. Younger students may review the resurrection of the body as well as the Apostles' Creed in their catechisms.

 Searching Scripture
Read the warnings of Scripture on the suddenness of death in Ecclesiastes 9:12, Matthew 25:13, Mark 13:32-37, 1 Thessalonians 5:1-11, and Revelation (Apocalypse) 3:3.

A Pilgrim's Prayer (Shrine of St. Anne in Beaupré)

The following prayer is the traditional prayer to St. Anne as prayed at the Shrine of St. Anne in Beaupré, located thirty miles east of the city of Quebec, Canada. Although you may never get to this shrine, if you have a special need you may spiritually place yourself before this miraculous shrine while reciting the following prayer.

A Pilgrim's Prayer

St. Anne, I have come to honor you and to call upon you in this blessed Shrine of Beaupré. Here, pilgrims have often felt some of the fruits of your goodness, power, and intercession. Like every true pilgrim, I also have favors to ask of you. I know that you will be as good to me as you have been, in the past, to thousands of others who have come to implore you in this Shrine.

St. Anne, you know the grace of which I stand most in need at the present moment, the special favor for which I have undertaken this pilgrimage. Hear my prayer. I entrust to your care, all of my material and spir-itual needs. I commend my family, my country, the Church, and the whole world to you. Keep me faithful to Christ and His Church, and one day escort me into the Father's Eternal Home. Amen.

Book Summary Test for *Blessed Marie of New France*

Directions: Answer in complete sentences. If necessary, use the back of the page for additional writing space. (100 possible points, 20 points for each answer)

1. What religious order did Blessed Marie enter? At what age did she enter? What made her different from most of the nuns at the convent?

2. What prompted Blessed Marie's desire to go to New France (Canada)? How long did she have to wait for this dream to come true?

3. Which of the native tribes were most friendly toward the French colonists and the Ursuline nuns? Which were the least friendly?

4. Briefly explain some the hardships endured by Blessed Marie as an Ursuline nun situated in Canada during its early days of settlement.

5. List some of Blessed Marie Guyart of the Incarnation's accomplishments. What examples of her heroic virtue can you give?

Blessed Marie of New France, The Story of the First Missionary Sisters in Canada
Answer Key to Comprehension Questions

Chapter 1—In Which Madame Marie Martin Joins the Ursulines
1. Archbishop Bertrand d'Eschaux, Archbishop of Tours, asked Madame Martin to visit him to discuss her vocation to the Ursuline convent.
2. As a child of seven, Madame Martin had a dream in which our Lord asked her to be His special friend. By the time she was fourteen, she felt called to become a nun.
3. Madame Martin was a thirty-year-old widow with an eleven-year-old boy when she entered the Ursuline convent.

Chapter 2—In Which Mère Marie Dreams of Becoming a Missionary
1. In her early days as an Ursuline nun, Sister Marie was distracted by her son's visits to the convent demanding that his mother come home.
2. The two trials that Sister Marie discussed with her Novice Mistress were her doubts of God's existence (which her Novice Mistress declared was a common trick of the devil), and Sister Marie's notion that God had work for her somewhere other than in the Ursuline convent at Tours, France.
3. From 1631 to 1632, Claude Martin was enrolled in the Jesuit boarding school at Rennes, from which he was dismissed as he did not show any interest in his studies. He was sent back to Tours and returned to school in 1633, this time with the Jesuits in Orlèans. He was more successful in Orlèans where he "endeared himself to everyone there" (page 22).
4. The Jesuits requested that teaching nuns be sent to New France in order to convert the Native American girls and to provide proper education and training for the children of the French colonists.

Chapter 3—In Which Mère Marie Waits for Her Dream to Come True
1. Madame Marie Madeleine de la Peltrie was a 37-year-old wealthy widow who lived in Alencon, France. She had a desire to use her fortune to educate the young girls in Canada.
2. Some of the hardships to be endured by missionaries to Canada included the long journey by ship to get there, the cold climate of the region, and the lack of nourishing, varied foods.
3. After waiting for four years to become a missionary to New France, Mère Marie was given only thirty-six hours to prepare to leave the Ursuline convent at Tours.

Chapter 4—In Which Mère Marie Tells Claude of Her Missionary Plans
1. In her attempt to keep Mère Marie from going to New France, Madame Buisson threatened both the Archbishop of Tours and the mayor. She also discontinued Claude Martin's payments for his room, board, and tuition at the Jesuit school in Orlèans; and sent a letter to Claude to tell him of his mother's plans in an attempt to turn Claude against his mother.
2. Her son, Claude—hurt and angry—was waiting for Mère Marie when she arrived at the inn in Orlèans.
3. Upon their arrival in Paris, Mère Marie and her companions received news that Claude Martin had decided to become a priest and was on his way to Paris for an interview with the Jesuit superiors.

Chapter 5—In Which Mère Marie Arrives in New France
1. The missionaries felt that their success in Canada depended chiefly upon their "faith in God—real faith—no matter what happens" (page 58).
2. Monsieur Bernières told Mère Marie that he would write or visit those who had promised to help the missionaries with prayers or money. He felt they might need a personal reminder as time went on.

3. On the way to New France, the *Saint Joseph* strayed northerly and nearly collided with a large iceberg.

Chapter 6—In Which Mère Marie and Her Companions Arrive in Quebec
1. Although the cargo of fish made the trip unpleasant, the "great consolation" that Mère Marie and her companions had while on board the *Saint Jacques* was "the chance to hear three more Masses each day" (page 75).
2. When Mère Marie arrived in 1639, the population of Quebec was around two hundred men, women, and children. (The November 2012 population of the city of Quebec, Canada, [according to the Quebec "population clock"] is 8,081,467 people.)
3. Upon their arrival in Quebec, the nuns were greeted by the entire populace, a formal address by the mayor, a procession to the church, fireworks, feasting, and a tour of the town.

Chapter 7—In Which Mère Marie Makes A Great Sacrifice
1. Père Le Jeune told Mère Marie that it was important to teach the children their Christian faith due to the nomadic lifestyle of the tribes. He felt that if the children were taught to know, love, and serve God from early childhood that they would be more likely to keep their Faith no matter where they went.
2. During the winter of 1639-40, smallpox broke out in New France.
3. In the spring of 1642, Madame de la Peltrie decided to move to Montreal, taking all her possessions as well as Charlotte with her. Mère Marie offered this sacrifice for her son and his priestly vocation.

Chapter 8—In Which the Ursulines Move into Their New Convent
1. Mère Marie was worried about Madame de la Peltrie in Montreal as word went out that the Iroquois tribe was planning to attack their enemy, the Huron tribe, in and around Montreal.
2. The Ursulines moved into their new convent—the house on the rock—on November 21, 1642.
3. Several events occurred that brought Madame de la Peltrie back to Quebec including the threat of the Iroquois attack on Montreal and Madame de la Peltrie's dangerous—and unpopular—idea to take a canoe and move into a Huron village to work as a missionary.

Chapter 9—In Which the Ursulines Oo Quebec Suffer Two Great Losses
1. Fire destroyed the Ursuline convent in Quebec on December 30, 1650.
2. After the fire, the Ursulines became entirely dependent upon the Augustinian nuns, relying on them for shelter, food, and clothing until moving into the house of Madame de la Peltrie in late January of 1651.
3. On April 4, 1652, Mère St. Joseph, the fun-loving Ursuline nun, died of tuberculosis. (To read Mère Marie's account of the life and death of Mère St. Joseph, go online to http://puffin.creighton.edu/jesuit/relations/relations_38.html, and read Chapter X.

Chapter 10—In Which the Iroquois Trouble the French Colonists
1. Mère Marie diplomatically convinced the bishop that she and three companions should remain at the fortified convent in order to prepare meals for the troops stationed there.
2. The bishop felt that the unrest between the Iroquois and the French colonists was the fault of the current French king, King Louis XIV, as the young king did not understand the French colonists' need for protection and was unwilling to send French troops to Canada.
3. Because of the peace that was established between the French colonists and the Iroquois nation, Jesuit missionaries were again able to preach the gospel in the vast wilderness south of the St. Lawrence (page 136). Mère Marie was hopeful that a further result would be that the Iroquois would send some of their children to her school in Quebec.

Chapter 11—In Which Mère Marie Is Taken to Her Heavenly Reward
1. Mère Marie disagreed with the French colonists' practice of trading liquor for beaver skins with the native tribes. (Another North American missionary, Venerable Frederic Baraga—the first bishop of the Diocese of Marquette, Michigan—also struggled with this issue. Read about

his life in RACE for Heaven's *By Cross and Anchor Study Edition, The Story of Frederic Baraga on Lake Superior*.)
2. In 1670, Mère Marie requested that she be allowed to step down as superior of the Ursuline community and that she be released from her current duties. From that time on, her duties consisted of hearing the children's catechism, writing letters back home to France, and teaching the younger nuns the native languages. (Note that throughout her life, Mère Marie wrote many letters to France, especially to her son Claude. Over 12,000 of her letters have survived. When a history of the French colonies was written in 1866, it relied heavily upon the letters of Mère Marie. Using in part these letters, her son Claude composed the first biography of Mère Marie of the Incarnation, which he wrote five years after her death. In 1681, he published 221 of her letters. Some of these letters may be read online at www.ursulines-uc.com/eng (then go to "Marie of the Incarnation" on the right and scroll down to her letters). Blessed Marie, at the direction of her confessor, also wrote an account of her spiritual life—often called her autobiography—which she sent to Claude. Also note that Mère Marie mastered three of the native languages and wrote simple catechisms in the Huron and Algonquin languages, a sacred history and collection of prayers in Algonquin, and a catechism and primitive dictionary in Iroquois—once again a strong parallel to the life of Venerable Bishop Frederic Baraga.)
3. Monsieur Talon attributed Dom Claude Martin's success as a scholar and priest to the prayers and sacrifices of Claude's mother, Blessed Marie of New France.

Answer Key to Book Summary Test

1. Marie Guyart entered the cloistered convent of the Ursulines at Tours, France, on January 25, 1631. Upon her entrance, she was a 31-year-old widow with an eleven-year-old son. Being previously married and a mother made her different from most of the other nuns at the convent.
2. Marie (who took the religious name of Marie of the Incarnation) desired to go to New France after experiencing a dream in which she saw the country of New France and had the Blessed Mother kiss her three times, beckoning her to come to that country to make her Son better known. Jesus also called her to this country asking her to "build a house for Jesus and Mary" (page 28). Blessed Marie was given a copy of the Jesuit *Relations* by one of Claude's teachers that described the missionary experiences of several Jesuit priests in New France. However, Blessed Marie had to wait for four years before sufficient financing was obtained to make this dream a reality.
3. The Huron tribe was the friendliest toward the French colonists and the Ursuline nuns, while the Iroquois were the least friendly.
4. Many hardships were endured by Blessed Marie as an Ursuline nun situated in Canada during its early days of settlement including the lack of nourishing, varied foods (Often cornmeal and dried fish were their only food.); the harsh climate of the region—ice and snow in the winter and heat in the summer; the long, difficult journey by ship to get there; the separation from relatives (such as Blessed Marie's son Claude); the constant threat of war with the Iroquois; and the language barrier.
5. Some of Blessed Marie's accomplishments include the following: she followed God's call to become a nun despite all obstacles; she braved the dangerous journey and living conditions of a wild country to establish a cloistered convent and school; she became fluent in several native languages, fluent enough to teach others and to write prayer books and catechisms in those languages; she found the time to write over 12,000 letters about her experiences and spiritual insights. Answers to the second question will vary.

Other RACE for Heaven Products

Catholic Study Guides for Mary Fabyan Windeatt's Saint Biography Series teach the Catholic faith to all members of your family. Written with your family's various learning levels in mind, these flexible study guides succeed as stand-alone unit studies or supplements to your regular curriculum. Thirty to sixty minutes per day will allow your family to experience:

- ☑ The spirituality and holy habits of the saints
- ☑ Lively family discussions on important faith topics
- ☑ Increased critical thinking and reading comprehension skills
- ☑ Quality read-aloud time with Catholic "living books"
- ☑ Enhanced knowledge of Catholic doctrine and the Bible
- ☑ History and geography incorporated into saintly literature
- ☑ Writing projects based on secular and Catholic historical events and characters

Purchase these guides individually or in the following grade-level packages. (Grade level is are determined solely on the length of each book in the series.)

Grades 3-4: *St. Thomas Aquinas, The Story of the "Dumb Ox"; St. Catherine of Siena, The Girl Who Saw Saints in the Sky; Patron Saint of First Communicants, The Story of Blessed Imelda Lambertini;* and *The Miraculous Medal, The Story of Our Lady's Appearances to St. Catherine Labouré*

Grade 5: *St. Rose, First Canonized Saint of the Americas; St. Martin de Porres, The Story of the Little Doctor of Lima, Peru; King David and His Songs, A Story of the Psalms;* and *Blessed Marie of New France, The Story of the First Missionary Sisters in Canada*

Grade 6: *St. Dominic, Preacher of the Rosary and Founder of the Dominicans; St. Benedict, The Story of the Father of the Western Monks; The Children of Fatima and Our Lady's Message to the World;* and *St. John Masias, Marvelous Dominican Gate-keeper of Lima, Peru*

Grade 7: *The Little Flower, The Story of St. Therese of the Child Jesus; St. Hyacinth, The Story of the Apostle of the North; The Curé of Ars, The Story of St. John Vianney, Patron Saint of Parish Priests;* and *St. Louis de Montfort, The Story of Our Lady's Slave*

Grade 8: *Pauline Jaricot, Foundress of the Living Rosary and the Society for the Propagation of Faith; St. Francis Solano, Wonder-Worker of the New World and Apostle of Argentina and Peru; St. Paul the Apostle, The Story of the Apostle to the Gentiles;* and *St. Margaret Mary, Apostle of the Sacred Heart*

The Windeatt Dictionary: Pre-Vatican II Terms and Catholic Words from Mary Fabyan Windeatt's Saint Biographies explains over 450 Catholic terms and expressions used in this popular saint biography series. Indispensable in expanding knowledge and practice of the Catholic faith, this book provides a ready access for the Catholic vocabulary words used in the RACE for Heaven Windeatt study guides. This dictionary also includes a Catholic book report resource that contains suggestions for forty-five Catholic book reports: fourteen writing projects, ten book report activities, and twenty-one topics for saint biographies.

Graced Encounters with Mary Fabyan Windeatt's Saints: 344 Ways to Imitate the Holy Habits of the Saints is a compilation of the "Growing in Holiness" sections of RACE for Heaven's Catholic study guides for the Windeatt saint biography series and presents 344 examples of saintly behavior, one for nearly every chapter in each of these twenty biographies. Enhance your encounter with the saints by practicing the models of devotion, service, penance, prayer, and virtue offered in this guide.

Bedtime Bible Stories for Catholic Children: Loving Jesus through His Word contains twenty discussions of Bible stories that were originally published in serial form in a Catholic children's magazine. Their author stated, "The tales are extremely simple and unadorned. They are real conversations of a real child and her mother." Due to popular demand, the series was later (1910) published as a book, *Bible Stories Told to "Toddles."* The engaging conversational style of this book lends itself well as a bedtime read-aloud that allows Jesus to come alive in the Gospels. The study aids include discussion questions to help foster spiritual conversation, Bible excerpts relevant to the presented story, "Growing in Holiness" suggestions for living the Gospel message in our daily lives, and short catechism lessons for both children and adults.

I Talk with God: The Art of Prayer and Meditation for Catholic Children strives to instill in young Catholics a love of prayer and a practical knowledge of the art of meditation. This prayer book contains prayers to pray out loud (vocal prayer) or in the silence of your heart. It shows how you can talk with God, and more importantly, how you can love God. As you progress through this book—from discovering what prayer is to reading and reciting simple prayers to understanding meditation and then to helps for deeper meditation—you will see that prayer and meditation often go together. Meditation is described by the big *Catechism of the Catholic Church* as nothing more than "prayerful reflection" or *holy thinking*. You can use books, devotions, pictures, holy cards, and images (such as the stained glass windows in church) to help you think about holy people, events, and ideas. Learn how to talk with God each day to increase your love for Him and follow more closely His holy will.

Communion with the Saints: A Family Preparation Program for First Communion and Beyond in the Spirit of St. Therese imitates St. Therese of the Child Jesus and her family who studied and prayed for sixty-nine days in anticipation of Therese's First Holy Communion. Modeling this preparation, the *Communion with the Saints* program will help any family find renewed fervor in the reception of the Eucharist. This resource includes a chapter-by-chapter study of the following four books:

- *The Little Flower, The Story of Saint Therese of the Child Jesus*—to provide the foundation of God's love for us and to encourage a desire for holiness

- *The Children of Fatima and Our Lady's Message to the World*—to show the sinfulness of our world and the need to avoid sin

- *The Patron Saint of First Communicants, The Story of Blessed Imelda Lambertini*—to inspire devotion to the Sacrament of Holy Communion

- *The King of the Golden City* by Mother Mary Loyola —to illustrate Jesus' Presence as a source of grace necessary to live a holy life

Each of the sixty-nine days of preparation includes read-aloud selections with enrichment activities, meditational readings, catechism lessons, and plenty of practical application to promote a growth in holiness and sanctity. Weekend suggestions include a list of over thirty-five family projects. The use of *My First Communion Journal* is encouraged with this program.

My First Communion Journal in Imitation of Saint Therese, The Little Flower provides a lasting keepsake of a child's First Holy Communion. This journal has been constructed in imitation of the copybook made for Therese Martin by her older sister Pauline to help Therese prepare for her First Holy Communion. Although this book is not an exact replica of the copybook used by Therese, it does contain many of the same prayers and aspirations she used, the same idea of flowers inspiring virtue, and the same method of recording prayers recited and sacrifices made. It is up to you to decorate and complete this journal, replicating Therese's heroic efforts by raising your mind and heart to Jesus and by humbling yourself with small sacrifices. Learn as well to imitate St. Therese's love and knowledge of Scripture as you meditate on—or even memorize—the biblical passages that are provided for reflection. This journal may be completed in conjunction with the *Communion with the Saints* program or used separately.

My First Communion Journal in Imitation of St. Paul, Putting on the Armor of God was also inspired by St. Therese's copybook and uses the same method of encouraging—and recording—daily prayers and mortifications. However, instead of using flowers to illustrate virtues, this resource uses the battle model St. Paul describes in Ephesians 6:10-17. First communicants are encouraged to arm themselves with virtues and spiritual weapons in order to fight as soldiers of Christ. The scriptural words of Jesus and St. Paul are reflected on frequently to encourage the imitation of the actions and love of Jesus and to inspire a love and knowledge of Holy Scripture. This journal too may be completed in conjunction with the *Communion with the Saints* program or used separately.

The King of the Golden City Study Edition is a new edition of a book that was originally published in 1921. This treasure of a book was written in response to a student's appeal for instructions along with "little stories" to help her prepare for Holy Communion. To fulfill this request, Mother Loyola of the Bar Convent in York, England, wrote a simple story that illustrates Jesus' desire to share an intimate relationship with each one of His children. This new edition contains some updated language but, quite deliberately, does not contain any pictures. Readers, as they progress through this story, will form a mental image of their King, one as unique and personal as their own relationship with Him. The study sections assist with the allegory, connect to the Bible as well as to the catechism, and explore the art of prayer in the spirit of the three Carmelite Doctors of the Church. Although written over ninety years ago for a young child, this book remains a timeless masterpiece of Catholic literature suitable for all ages. (Also available as a study guide only)

The Good Shepherd and His Little Lambs Study Edition is a simply told Catholic tale of four children who meet with their beloved aunt for "First Communion talks." More than a story, it is a First Communion primer that takes the tenets of the catechism and, through naturally-flowing conversations, relates them in the language of little ones to authentic Christian living. As Mrs. Bosch explains, "We might learn the catechism all the way through beautifully, and at the end find ourselves still very stiff and clumsy about loving our Lord. When He comes to us, we don't want to welcome Him into our souls only with answers out of the catechism, do we?" Enriched by appropriate Biblical passages, points of doctrine, and prayers, this story-primer is an enjoyable and effective read-aloud that will prepare the Good Shepherd's little lambs to worthily receive Him in the Holy Eucharist.

A Reconciliation Reader-Retreat: Read-Aloud Lessons, Stories, and Poems for Young Catholics Preparing for Confession provides a basic doctrinal explanation and review of the Sacrament of Reconciliation as well as a Gospel examination of conscience—a seven-day read-aloud formation retreat. To help the lessons come alive and to enable young Catholics to more readily apply these doctrines to their own daily lives, the lessons have been supplemented with pertinent short stories and poems. Each lesson contains reflection questions, a family prayer, and a "Gospel Examination of Conscience" that is formulated according to the dictates of the *Catechism of the Catholic Church*. This reader-retreat will not only enrich and deepen the sacramental experience for each member of your family but it will also provide several tools to help you recommit to leading a virtuous life and to grow together in holiness.

Devotion to St. Joseph: Read-Aloud Stories, Poems, and Prayers for Catholic Children encourages children to love Jesus as St. Joseph did. As Scripture does not record a single word this great saint spoke; we must take our lessons of his life from his actions. In this compilation of stories and poems about our Savior's foster-father from renowned Catholics, children of all ages are encouraged to imitate the virtues the life of St. Joseph reveal to us in his loving dedication to Jesus and Mary. The discussion questions as well as the reflections on the virtues of St. Joseph lead children to apply the lessons of this saint's life to their own while the prayer section promotes a lasting devotion to the great St. Joseph. As St. Teresa of Avila declared, "I wish I could persuade everyone to be devoted to this glorious saint!"

The Month of St. Joseph: Prayers and Practices for Each Day of March in Imitation of the Virtues of St. Joseph was originally published in 1874. This book contains daily meditations on the life and virtues of St. Joseph for adults and high-school students. In addition, each day presents a prayer to St. Joseph, several resolutions, a short ejaculatory prayer, a relevant Scripture verse, and a brief consideration for reflection. The practices for each day are intended to assist the reader in acquiring the habits of prayer and interior recollection so necessary to living in the presence of God. Perfect for Lenten reading, this journey through the life of St. Joseph reveals his love of God and neighbor, humility, quiet action, and spirit of sacrifice. While the Bible tells so little about St. Joseph's life, here we discover the abundant virtues of this silent saint—and are challenged to imitate them.

Alternative Book Reports for Catholic Students contains forty-five book report ideas to encourage critical thinking for ages seven to fourteen. These ideas are intended to provoke a reflection on those themes and topics that support and encourage Catholic living as well as some that may conflict with our Faith. Many report topics require an examination of our personal faith life and prompt us to take lessons from the saints to strengthen our own faith in God. The suggested activities vary from written exercises to creative art projects and include twenty-one topics specifically designed for saint biographies. Other activities can be used within a group or family.

Reading the Saints: Lists of Catholic Books for Children Plus Book Collecting Tips for the Home and School Library (formerly entitled *Saintly Resources*) is a valuable tool for Catholic home educators, classroom teachers, and collectors of Catholic juvenile books. This resource will help you discover living books from such popular out-of-print Catholic juvenile series as Catholic Treasury, Vision Books, and American Background Books as well as current series books for young Catholics. Use this book to find:

- Over 800 Catholic books listed by author, series, reading level, century, and geographical location
- More than 275 authors of saint biographies, historical fiction, and poetry written for Catholic juvenile readers
- Publishers of Catholic children's books, present and past
- Helpful advice for collecting and caring for used books
- Hundreds of age-appropriate, accessible living books to enrich your study of the Catholic Church's rich heritage of saints and notable Catholic historical figures
- Information on how to build and maintain your own library of Catholic juvenile books
- Inspiring quotations about book collecting, reading, and the love of books

The Outlaws of Ravenhurst Study Edition contains a classic story of the persecution of Scottish Catholics that was first written in 1923 and was revised and reprinted in 1950. This 2009 edition of Sr. M. Imelda Wallace's *Outlaws of Ravenhurst* contains the revised story of 1950 plus chapter-by-chapter aids to assist readers in assimilating the book's strong Catholic elements into their own lives. The study section focuses on critical thinking, integration of biblical teachings, and the study of the virtuous life to which Christ calls us as mature Catholics. With its emphasis on virtues (theological and moral plus the gifts and fruits of the Holy Spirit), the spiritual and corporal works of mercy, and the Beatitudes, *Outlaws of Ravenhurst Study Edition* is a fun and effective catechetical tool for Catholics preparing for the Sacrament of Confirmation. (Also available as a study guide only)

The Family that Overtook Christ Study Edition: The Story of the Family of St. Bernard of Clairvaux is an excellent read for young adults who are preparing to receive the Sacrament of Confirmation. In this exciting chronicle of the life of twelfth-century knights, we have an entire family of nine saints who lay before us their individual means of achieving intimate union with Christ. Learn with the Fontaines family how to supernaturalize the natural, develop a God-consciousness, and attain sanctity by being yourself. Perfect for high-school read-aloud (or adult study), this new study edition has over 250 footnotes for increased comprehension and provides discussion/meditation points to promote the art of spiritual conversation. The appendix lists formulas of Catholic doctrine that are essential for confirmands not only to know but also to incorporate into their own spiritual lives.

A Confirmation Reader-Retreat: Read-Aloud Lessons, Stories and Poems for Young Catholics utilizes chapters from two excellent out-of-print Catholic books for children (*I Belong to God, Great Truths in Simple Stories for Children and Lovers of Children* by Lillian Clark; and *Children's Retreats in Preparation for First Confession, First Holy Communion, and Confirmation* by Rev. P.A. Halpin). This book provides a basic doctrinal review of the Sacrament of Confirmation as well as prayer experiences—a nine-day read-aloud retreat/novena. The reprinted material has been supplemented with short stories and poems that provide insights in applying catechetical doctrines to the daily life of young Catholics. Each lesson concludes with "I Talk with God"—a section that encourages readers (of all ages) to deepen their relationship with each of the Three Persons of the Blessed Trinity. Reflection questions promote the habit of spiritual conversation within your family—to encourage family members to discuss holy topics—and to help you grow together in holiness. Additionally, a traditional novena to the Holy Spirit is included.

By Cross and Anchor Study Edition: The Story of Frederic Baraga on Lake Superior relates the exciting, and often miraculous, missionary adventures of the "Snowshoe Priest"—Venerable Frederic Baraga, the first bishop of Michigan's Upper Peninsula. Declared "Venerable" by Pope Benedict XVI on May 10, 2012, this priest came to the United States from Slovenia in 1830 to undertake his mission as a "simple servant of God." For almost forty years, Fr. Frederic Baraga traveled across over 80,000 square miles of wilderness by snowshoe in winter and canoe in summer. In imitation of Christ, Bishop Baraga become poor so that he might bring the riches of the Catholic Faith to the Chippewa and immigrant residents of the beautiful peninsula he served. Although not strictly a biography, this book is a story based on historical facts drawn from Bishop Baraga's own journal and letters—a fascinating, easy-to-read history of Michigan's northern peninsula. While this exciting adventure is intended for youth who are interested in knowing more about this quiet, courageous priest, readers of all ages will be inspired by his life of humility, simplicity, and selfless virtue. This new study edition contains over 130 footnotes, defining less familiar vocabulary words and—gleaned from Venerable Baraga's *Journal* and other primary sources—details regarding the region's people and places. Also included are discussion questions, applicable Scripture passages, pertinent quotations of Venerable Baraga from the text, and—most importantly—a section illustrating how to imitate the various virtues of Venerable Frederic Baraga. Additionally, the complete text of Bishop Baraga's 1853 "Pastoral Letter to the Faithful" has been included with numerous references added in order that we may read this in light of Scripture and the *Compendium of the Catechism of the Catholic Church.* Learn more about the life, ministry, and heroic virtues of Venerable Frederic Baraga, the "Snowshoe Priest."

To Order: Email info@RACEforHeaven.com or place an order at RACEforHeaven.com. Discover, MasterCard, VISA, PayPal, American Express, checks, and money orders are accepted.

www.ingramcontent.com/pod-product-compliance
Lightning Source LLC
Chambersburg PA
CBHW081841170426

43199CB00017B/2808